Beholding Jesus

Letters to My Children

John D. Gillespie

Myrrh Books
Overland Park, Kansas

Beholding Jesus
© 2013, 2019 John D. Gillespie

Published by Myrrh Books
Overland Park, Kansas

ISBN: 9781795717212
Library of Congress Control Number: 2001012345

Printed in the United States of America

Dedication

To your Aunt Nell,
Who has prayerfully followed your lives:
Rejoicing over you
Weeping with you
Believing the best about you.

"A woman who fears the Lord is to be praised."
(Proverbs 31:30)

About the Author

John and Tessa Gillespie have been married for thirty-one years. They have seven children and a stream of grandchildren. While John has been a pastor in the UK and the USA for thirty years, his greatest desire is that his family and home reflect the grace and truth of the Gospel and the mission values of the Kingdom of God.

John now travels to pastors in the Majority World in a training and encouragement ministry with Global Training Network. When not travelling, together with Tessa, John enjoys walking, cycling, barbecuing, and pouring his heart into his children and grandchildren.

Having lived in England for twenty-six years, John and Tessa now reside in Overland Park, Kansas.

Table of Contents

A Warm Welcome

Dear Friends,

No doubt, you were taught (quite properly) that it is rude to read someone else's mail. Most of the time, this would be appropriate. But in the case of this book, I welcome you to read my letters to my children.

My wife and I have had a grace-filled, riotous journey raising our family. There have been many tears and much laughter, much fighting and forgiving, countless trips to the cross, endless hours of discussion, debate, argument, frustration and breakthroughs over the years. But I can say, in truth, that the trademark of our home has been the constant presence of Jesus, by His Word, and in His grace (and I think our kids would agree). Tessa and I have tried to be deliberate in imparting to our seven children the wonders of God and His Gospel. Alas, we have so often faltered and failed! Our children have seen the very worst of us, but it has been precisely at those times when Jesus has shone through in all of His grace and goodness.

It is my concern that my children know what I believe about Jesus Christ before I leave this planet. I do not want to leave them in any doubt as to what I have come to discover of Him in the Bible. He has been, is, and forever shall be, the passion of my life. Hence these letters: I have written thirty, but could have written 100. The wonders of Jesus are without number (John 21:25). These letters are deliberately written with a minimum of "editing." I wanted them to be written expressions of the heart, as letters are. You will find more thorough Christologies, written by those more capable than I. Take these for what they are, and if you find some blessing in them, then I am pleased. When you find better, I won't mind.

Our years of raising our children went by so quickly! Yes, we had to deal with most all of the trials and attacks that come upon a modern family. I need not name them, for you know them too. Ours was not a sterile home. You never found our family pictured—all smiles and neatly pressed—on the front of your favourite Christian magazine. But through it all, the Lord Jesus was constantly calling us back to Himself.

Some of you sat at our table. That is where most of "life" happened for us. That is where we feasted, fought (oh the fights!), and forgave. Our kids met inspiring people as guests around our table. We always seemed to have some missionary, tramp, dynamic friend, or fledgling follower seated with us. That table is where we opened the Bible, debated Christian things, and "did" our theology. Then there was Story Time. Night after night, we gathered as Mom read from the lives of the great and simple. Together we drank in the inspiring stories of those who lived their years for Jesus. Even the teenage buddies of our sons were heard to say, "Hey Mrs. G! Are we in time for stories?" Through it all, we saw young lives being shaped for and by Jesus Christ. Today, when we manage to gather, Story Time is still a highlight.

Most of our children are raised and gone now. The grandkids are coming, and the generations are being formed. I wrote these letters for them as well, that they might know what their grandparents believed. Tessa and I, faltering disciples of a wonderful Saviour, always desired more than to just eke out a Christian existence. Our desire was to sow love for Jesus and His Gospel into the generations that follow, that they will grow stronger with them. My wife and I have seven wonderful children, but we have many spiritual sons and daughters, brothers, and sisters—too many to name. You know who you are. These letters are for you as well. Take them as from my heart to yours.

> He decreed statutes for Jacob
> and established the law in Israel,
> which he commanded our ancestors
> to teach their children,

so the next generation would know them,
even the children yet to be born,
and they in turn would tell their children.

Then they would put their trust in God
and would not forget his deeds
but would keep his commands.
(Psalm 78:5-7)

Introduction

My Dear Children,

This is a book for you, about Jesus. It is my heart's desire to share some of the wonders of Jesus Christ with you. It has been such a joy to be your father, to see you all grow, develop your wings, and fly away. Each one of you has a special place in my heart that no one else can or ever will replace. For us, you truly have been "arrows in the hands of a warrior" (Psalm 127:3) your mother and I sent from the tightly strung bows of our hearts, to places near and far. Through you, our little lives are bearing fruit for Christ in continents, countries, and cultures where we ourselves could only dream of sharing Jesus.

Your mom and I consecrated ourselves to the service of Jesus on the day we were engaged...on a lonely highway in the middle of the Boston Mountains. God gave us grace to see His Son as our treasure, and His Kingdom and cause as worth everything. Since that day we have seen our marriage summed up in 2 Corinthians 4:5, in the words of the Apostle Paul:

> For what we preach is not ourselves, but Jesus Christ as Lord, and ourselves as your servants for Jesus' sake.

That text was once inscribed on the inside of my wedding ring. The inscription has long worn off the gold, but not off our hearts. For although we were truly in love (and still are now),[1] we have seen that Christian marriage must exist for something greater than itself, or it will turn towards idolatry. It must essentially exist for the glory of Christ.

Each of you were conceived and cherished with the conscious and constant prayer that you, each and all, would live your lives for Jesus, be givers and not takers, be part of the solution and not part of the problem in this desperate world. We prayed day and night that your lives would be meaningful for the Kingdom, and rich towards God. We asked God to make you missionaries, mission-minded, lovers of good, haters of evil, fascinated by Christ, soldiers, givers, goers, peace-loving fighters. We asked that your lives be measured not by duration, but by donation, not by bank balances, but by extravagance towards others, not by comfort, but by sacrificial effectiveness.

We prayed for your spouses from the time you were infants, that God would bring His choice into your lives, that your marriages would be marked by fidelity to Jesus and His Gospel and to each other, that your marriages would reflect something of the love Jesus has for His Church.

God is answering the prayers of our hearts.

We kept ever before us the countless Bible promises from God for you as our children. In prayers from my heart, I constantly reached to God's Word; perhaps to no passage more than Psalm 112:1-2, especially during times of trial, when various ones of you wandered or struggled, or when Satan was trying to ruin you. It reads:

> Praise the L<small>ORD</small>.
>
> Blessed are those who fear the L<small>ORD</small>,
> who find great delight in his commands.
>
> Their children will be mighty in the land;
> the generation of the upright will be blessed.

That psalm led me to a thousand heart "searchings," ("Am I a *man who fears the Lord?*"), and to pound upon Heaven's door a thousand times for your lives and souls.

How faithful the Lord has been!

So this book is written as my heart-gift to you. It is not about you. It is about Jesus Christ. It is part of my legacy to you. It has been written with tears and joys, in airplanes, my study, and on the sofa during Story Time (Mom always asking me to "pay attention"). You will know from being in your mother and father's home, that:

What you think about when you think about Jesus is the most important thing about you.

I believe passionately in sound theology. I believe that God has made Himself known in Jesus Christ, and that the Bible is His faithful record of that self-disclosure. I believe that this next century will be one in which being faithful to the Jesus of the Bible will be the biggest battle the Church will face. I believe that the world has no hope if the Church does not faithfully offer Christ, and if believers have not faithfully lived out the Gospel *in every generation*.

So it is your mother's and my prayer that you will all *go deep with Jesus*, repudiate the shallowness and triviality of our age, and know Him who is life itself. I pray night and day that as you treasure Him supremely, you will not hold your brief lives as dear. I pray that the wise words of Jim Elliot (one of my heroes) will also be yours:

> He is no fool, who gives what he cannot keep to gain what he cannot lose.

The following chapters do not follow any systematic order, though they do form a Christology of sorts. I wrote them in the sequence they flowed from my heart, with a minimum of stopping and researching. In this sense, they are a bit raw and unrefined. They reflect the lifetime of a faltering disciple, husband, father, pastor, and sinner, dwelling upon Jesus. Take them as they come, and go further with Christ than I ever have.

I've put a hymn at the end of every chapter for three reasons: To help you meditate upon Christ as presented in the chapter, to help you and your generation see the richness of our hymnody (for fear that it is being lost), and to share with you hymns that have enriched my spiritual formation. Great thinking and right believing will produce the highest praise, the deepest worship, and the most significant living. So, meditate on these great hymns of our heritage, and keep them alive in your hearts and homes.

Your Father

Delhi Airport
February 2013

Unto you, therefore, which believe, He is precious. (1 Peter 2:7, KJV)

****

All Creatures of Our God and King,

All creatures of our God and King,
lift up your voices, let us sing:
Alleluia, alleluia!
Thou burning sun with golden beams,
thou silver moon that gently gleams,

O praise him, O praise him,
Alleluia, alleluia, alleluia!

Thou rushing wind that art so strong,
ye clouds that sail in heaven along,
O praise him, Alleluia!
Thou rising morn, in praise rejoice,
ye lights of evening, find a voice,

Thou flowing water, pure and clear,
make music for thy Lord to hear,

Alleluia, alleluia!
Thou fire so masterful and bright,
that givest man both warmth and light

Dear mother earth, who day by day
unfoldest blessings on our way,
O praise him, Alleluia!
The flowers and fruits that in thee grow,
let them his glory also show

And all ye men of tender heart,
forgiving others, take your part,
O sing ye Alleluia!
Ye who long pain and sorrow bear,
praise God and on him cast your care

And thou, most kind and gentle death,
waiting to hush our latest breath,
O praise him, Alleluia!
Thou leadest home the child of God,
and Christ our Lord the way hath trod

Let all things their Creator bless,
and worship him in humbleness,
O praise him, Alleluia!
Praise, praise the Father, praise the Son,
and praise the Spirit, Three in One

O praise him, O praise him,
Alleluia, alleluia, alleluia!
(St. Francis of Assisi, 1182-1226)

Letter 1

Behold the One Who Wants to Be Beheld

Father, I desire that they also whom thou hast given me be with me where I am, that they may behold my glory. John 17:24 (ASV)

Dear Ones,

The Jesus of the Bible (that is, the true and real Jesus) is not in hiding. He is not hard to find. Christianity is an "open secret." It is a mystery made plain. Jesus wants us to know and rejoice in Him. He is the very self-disclosure of the Eternal God:

> The Son is the radiance of God's glory and the exact representation of his being... (Hebrews 1:3)

> For in Christ all the fullness of the Deity lives in bodily form... (Colossians 2:9)

> No one has ever seen God, but the one and only Son, who is himself God and is in closest relationship with the Father, has made him known. (John 1:18)

It is true that we will never *exhaustively* know the Lord. How could we? He is infinite, we are finite; He is the Author of Life, we borrow life from Him; He is the Creator, we are but creatures. But this does not mean we cannot *truly* know the Lord. This does not mean that we cannot *significantly* know the Lord. This does not mean we cannot *expansively* know the Lord. In Jesus' prayer to His Father, on the last night of His earthly life, He prayed a petition which so beautifully revealed His heart towards us:

> Father, I want those you have given me to be with me where I am and to see my glory... (John 17:24)

Look at that word, "see." Jesus wants us to "see" His glory. I prefer the old word, "behold." This is the word used in the King James Version. Two things about this word are very significant to me. First, the tense: It is the *present subjunctive active,* which means a continuous, repeated action, something ongoing. Second, the meaning: It means "to gaze," with a sense of participation. Dwell on this: Jesus, the Son of God, co-equal and co-eternal with the Father and the Spirit, wants His redeemed people (that includes *us*), to:

- Be with Him in Glory, where He is
- Continuously and without cessation, gaze upon and participate in His very glory (the glory He had before the world began)

This is our destiny in Jesus! This is the will of Jesus Christ for us! Jesus died for our sins upon the cross; yes to save us from a deserved Hell, but more to fit us for an undeserved Heaven with Him! No other "religion" dares to conceive of such a grand plan. Don't accept any substitutes. Instead, spend and be spent in living that others may hear the Gospel and enter into life with Christ.

I believe that the love song in the Bible, Song of Songs, displays the romance of the Gospel. (It needs to be read alongside Romans, which displays the mechanics of the Gospel). There is a verse in this love song that tells us something of what *we* do to Jesus when we look lovingly His way:

> You have stolen my heart, my sister, my bride;
> you have stolen my heart
> with one glance of your eyes,
> with one jewel of your necklace.
> (Song of Songs 4:9)

Imagine that we can capture the very heart of Jesus with one glance of our eyes! What an amazing Saviour! He who needs *nothing* has *chosen to need us!* He who is infinitely beautiful and worthy has decided to desire us, and to be moved by our affections towards Him. We who are naturally diseased, defiled, and dead, have been healed, cleansed, and made alive by the choice and grace of our Bridegroom, that we might be His chosen Bride, who captivates His heart. Receive it, rejoice in it, and respond to it.

The Christian concept of Heaven is not the sensual paradise for which our Muslim friends hope. (And Allah is nowhere to be found there.) Nor is it the shapeless nirvana of the Buddhist (indeed, the word "nirvana" means, "blown out," as a candle). How sad! Nor is it the endless curse of rebirths from which our Hindu neighbours seek deliverance. (Jesus can deliver them!) The Christian is destined for Jesus Christ Himself, out of these "shadow-lands" and into the weight of glory itself. There will be no dullness, no boredom, but rather a worshipful life of discovery, service, relationship, and amazement, all themed on Jesus Christ.

Now, I must tell you a secret about myself. I struggle greatly with a cold, dispassionate heart. I wonder, how can this be so, when my destiny is to be with Jesus Christ? How I long for a heart aflame, and how thankful I am for those moments, sometimes ever so brief (at times, lasting a little while longer), when I actually *feel* my heart and soul embracing my destiny in Christ! But many are the days when I can relate very well to the confession of John Newton:

> Weak is the effort of my heart, and cold my warmest thought, but when I see Thee as Thou art, I'll praise thee as I ought!

Notice the hunger in that verse and heed a warning: Don't fool yourself. If there is no hunger in you now to know Christ (be it ever so small), expressed at least in some desire (be it ever so weak), producing at least some effort (be it ever so feeble), to seek Jesus Christ here and now (with Bible and heart open), then it is sheer presumption to assume that suddenly, at death, you will be "magically" transformed into someone who loves Jesus and wants to know Him.

Nevertheless, while you certainly can (and must) truly begin to behold Jesus Christ now, even your *best* times in worship, your *fondest* moments with Jesus, are *but a foretaste* of what is ahead for you. This truth needs to motivate us towards increasingly sacrificial, kingdom living. Check it out for yourselves and you will find that the most joyful, useful saints in history have been those who yearned and hungered for the eternal courts of their God. The truth of who Jesus Christ is and what He has in store for us needs to move us towards joyous abandon in living for Him. Just consider the wonders of our salvation, a justification purchased by the glorious Gospel, which not only pardons our sins, but clothes us in the very righteousness of Christ and bids us "come."

As I write these words, I am also reading a new biography of Dietrich Bonhoeffer, another one of my heroes. He followed Jesus right under the scrutiny of the Nazis in Germany. He was sent to Buchenwald concentration camp in February 1945 for his involvement in a plot to assassinate Hitler, and was hanged at Flossenburg on April 9.[2] The last he was heard to say were these epic words:

This is the end—for me the beginning of Life.

He was only thirty-nine years old. This young man could easily have saved himself by keeping quiet, by being inconspicuous, by staying away from Germany. But it was his life as a disciple of Jesus, and his confidence in the Gospel, his eye for eternity, which gave him the confidence he needed to fight for the innocent, to oppose the wicked, and to finally die in hope. He actually ran towards the battle, returning "to Germany from America in the summer of 1939, on the last free trans-Atlantic ocean-liner before the War, knowing full well that he was sailing to his death, but having decided that the choice was between bringing down the Third Reich or bringing down Christian civilization."[3] He was armed with the love of Christ and the hope of Heaven, and gave himself for others.

Don't forget your destiny in Christ. More than that, *glory* in it! Richard Baxter, when told he had six months to live, began to earnestly meditate upon Heaven. The result was the *800,000* word book, *The Saints' Everlasting Rest*.[4] Baxter recovered and lived another thirty years, but not before he learned to meditate half an hour a day on Heaven. We will do well if we learn to meditate five minutes a day on our glorious destiny!

Take a few minutes and worship Jesus Christ as you use the words of this ancient hymn to help you meditate upon Him:

****

How Sweet the Name of Jesus Sounds

How sweet the Name of Jesus sounds
In a believer's ear!
It soothes his sorrows, heals his wounds,
And drives away his fear.

It makes the wounded spirit whole,
And calms the troubled breast;
'Tis manna to the hungry soul,
And to the weary, rest.

Dear Name, the Rock on which I build,
My Shield and Hiding Place,
My never failing treasury, filled
With boundless stores of grace!

By Thee my prayers acceptance gain,
Although with sin defiled;
Satan accuses me in vain,
And I am owned a child.

Jesus! my Shepherd, Husband, Friend,
O Prophet, Priest and King,

My Lord, my Life, my Way, my End,
Accept the praise I bring.

Weak is the effort of my heart,
And cold my warmest thought;
But when I see Thee as Thou art,
I'll praise Thee as I ought.

Till then I would Thy love proclaim
With every fleeting breath,
And may the music of Thy Name
Refresh my soul in death!
(John Newton, 1725-1807)[5]

Letter 2

Behold the One in Whom Are Hidden All the Treasures of Wisdom and Knowledge

In whom are hidden all the treasures of wisdom and knowledge.
Colossians 2:3

Dearest Children,

We will spend eternity enraptured by the magnificence of Jesus. Indeed, our most intelligent words today, our deepest thoughts, our highest praises are but infant musings, real though they be, compared to what we will know, experience, and express when in His presence.

Have you ever considered that in *Jesus*, as in no one else, exists all "treasure" of every type, beauty of every form, every hue of colour, and every truth of knowledge? How thrilling is the Lord! All science, art, creativity, intellect, philosophy, beauty, mathematics, theology—you name it—*all the treasures of wisdom and knowledge* are hidden (known by and resolved) in *Him*.

Take some time and ponder this. Chew on it. Lean into it. Worship Jesus for who He is: The sole possessor of "all the treasures" of wisdom and knowledge. This means, as Francis Schaeffer rightly observed, that there will be "no final conflict" where truth is concerned. Science and faith (*true* science and *true* faith) will finally meet in Jesus Christ. All that is beautiful, artful, and true will finally find resolution and completion in Jesus Christ.

Mankind foolishly boasts of himself and his minuscule achievements. We make heroes of fools and gods of wood and stone. We consider ourselves to be the holders of wisdom and knowledge, all the while ignoring the one who holds not only all truth in Himself, but our very lives in His hands. We would do well to heed the Word of the Lord, spoken by the prophet:

> This is what the Lord says:
> 'Let not the wise boast of their wisdom
> or the strong boast of their strength
> or the rich boast of their riches,
> but let the one who boasts boast about this:
> that they have the understanding to know me,
> that I am the Lord, who exercises kindness,
> justice and righteousness on earth,
> for in these I delight, declares the Lord.
> (Jeremiah 9:23)

In my younger life, I never bothered to read much, including the Bible. To my shame, I admit that I basically bluffed my way through undergrad and graduate school with a bare minimum of reading. I was "evangelical," but certainly not on fire. Then when I was twenty-four or twenty-five, and pastoring in Hickory Plains, Arkansas, God began to really get ahold of my heart *and* mind (largely through the volcanic ministry of Keith Green). I developed an appetite for truth I had not known before. Later that year, on our honeymoon, Mom and I managed to take along not only our Bibles, but *Strong's Exhaustive Concordance* and a few A.W. Tozer books as well. (I also took two guitars. What an understanding mother you have!) I began to discover that when I read the Bible I was encountering Jesus, not exhaustively, but genuinely.[6] Jesus and I have for years now met daily in His Word, and together we are taking these first steps of our eternal journey. He goes slowly so that I can keep up. God has graciously given me an insatiable desire to read good books about Jesus and to discover Him in the Bible.[7] This is all God's grace to me. I have set it as my goal to know Him in all the fullness that I can this side of Heaven, even as

I expectantly yearn for the completeness that seeing Him will bring. *The Jesus of the Bible thrills me!*

The more I read of Him and encounter Him in the Bible, the more I think, *I just have to see this Jesus face to face. I must spend eternity with Him!* Can you imagine being in Glory with Jesus Christ, the Son of God, very God of very God, and, with glorified capacities, discovering, learning, creating, worshipping, dancing, singing, thinking, writing, playing, cooking—all with the one in whom are "all the treasures of wisdom and knowledge"?

I often think of Mary, one who so passionately loved and desired Jesus that she found herself at the tomb on that dark Resurrection Sunday. She just had to see Jesus. Not expecting to see Him alive, she nevertheless yearned to see Him, even if dead. John tells us that she actually saw two angels (John 20:12). Many if not most would have been thrilled and satisfied with such a sight, but not dear Mary. For her, two live angels did not match one dead Jesus. "Where is my Lord?" was her plea to the angels. Her yearning heart was more than satisfied...not by finding a Jesus in a shroud, but her Lord risen in life. Mary's experience tells us that when we truly seek after Christ, we can be sure to have our deepest longings not just met, but exceeded beyond what we ever dreamed.

There is a real sense that you get what you want from life. If you want little, you get little. If you are happy with shallow, you get shallow. Do not allow yourself to be satisfied with a bit of surface religiosity, a little second-hand knowledge of Christ. Accept no substitutes for *knowing Him.* It is in Christ that your deepest God-given abilities and longings will find their consummation. It is in Christ that you will become the true person God intended when He created and redeemed you. Every blessing in the Christian life flows from your relationship with Jesus.

Ask the Holy Spirit to help you understand the Bible and to discover Jesus in depth within its sacred pages. Ask that you may gain a true hunger for Jesus. Be certain that God the Father wants you to be fascinated by His Son. Guard your heart against all lesser loves. Dare to ask God to make you *jealously* His. Trust Him, that if He draws you especially close to His side, taking unusual concern for you in relation to Him, that you will be all the richer for it. His love for you may keep you tethered to Him in such a way that other Christians seem to have temporal freedoms that Christ denies you. That is okay. Seek to be satisfied in Christ as your "enough," and you will discover treasures about Him that the more casual and carefree never find.

Do not worry that you will ever, in the longest eternity, exhaust the wisdom and knowledge of Jesus and get bored. The most memorable sight I have ever beheld on this planet is the Grand Canyon. People stand transfixed, speechless, for hours as they gaze into its beauty and majesty. Yet it is but a scratch in the skin of the earth. In fact, if this celestial ball could be reduced to the size of a cue ball, you would not be able to feel the Grand Canyon with your fingertip. Still, it humbles us and captures our adoration for durations. Imagine what Jesus Christ will do to our glorified selves when we see Him who spoke the Grand Canyon, and all that there is, into being!

> For from him and through him and for him are all things.
> To him be the glory forever! Amen. (Romans 11:36)

The hymn below is one I recall from my childhood in Brazil (rarely sung today). I remember being scarcely able to see over the pew in front, snug between my young parents, singing these precious words:

****

Fairest Lord Jesus

> Fairest Lord Jesus, Ruler of all nature,
> O Thou of God and man the Son,
> Thee will I cherish, Thee will I honor,
> Thou, my soul's glory, joy and crown.

Fair are the meadows, fairer still the woodlands,
Robed in the blooming garb of spring;
Jesus is fairer, Jesus is purer,
Who makes the woeful heart to sing.

Fair is the sunshine, fairer still the moonlight,
And all the twinkling starry host;
Jesus shines brighter, Jesus shines purer
Than all the angels heaven can boast.

All fairest beauty, heavenly and earthly,
Wondrously, Jesus, is found in Thee;
None can be nearer, fairer or dearer,
Than Thou, my Savior, art to me.

Beautiful Savior! Lord of all the nations!
Son of God and Son of Man!
Glory and honor, praise, adoration,
Now and forever more be Thine.
(Origin uncertain, translated by Joseph
August Seiss,1823-1904)

Letter 3

Behold the One Who Bids Us Follow

My Sheep listen to my voice, I know them, and they follow me.
John 10:27

Dear Children,

When it is all over, when my days on earth are finished, I want to be remembered as a "follower of Jesus." That will be enough. Sure, I want you to know that I was orthodox, a pastor, a missionary, but really I just want to be known as one of the company who followed after Christ.

What else do you want as a description for your life? What else matters? To be a follower of the Shepherd-Lamb, to live (and have lived) with one's eyes fixed upon the one whom the Father sent to be our Saviour, certainly this is the highest accolade, the most noble title, the greatest privilege one can know: to be known as and called a "follower of Jesus."

Consider with me the wonders of a God who bids sinners to follow Him. This is the one who did "not come to call the righteous, but sinners" (Mark 2:17), who summoned the fishermen at Galilee with the simple, effective call: "Follow me, and I will make you fishers of men" (Matthew 4:19, KJV). It is He who unashamedly challenges us with the command, "Whoever wants to be my disciple must deny themselves and take up their cross daily and follow me." (Luke 9:23). He is the one who then embraces us with the promise, "Whoever follows me will never walk in darkness, but will have the light of life" (John 8:12). And what a motley crew responded! In fact, Jesus once said that His ministry was proven genuine in that:

The blind receive sight, the lame walk, those who have leprosy are cleansed, the deaf hear, the dead are raised, and the good news is proclaimed to the poor. (Matthew 11:5)

What company our Saviour keeps!

Early in my Christian life, Bonhoeffer's life-changing book, *The Cost of Discipleship* came into my hands. How I wore out the pages of that book! That very copy is in my hands again, now. To this day, I can remember going back into the cornfield behind your Grandfather Hines' home with this volcanic book in my hands, kneeling down between the cornrows, praying as I read its remarkable pages. It was in the introduction to this book, right there on the first page, that I read these words:

When Christ calls a man, He bids him come and die.

These words went straight into my heart, but they did not bypass my mind. They provoked me, prodded me, investigated me...they still do today. For we follow not only our gentle Saviour, but our Lord as well. And yes, it is costly to follow Jesus Christ, for while He bids us to freely come, He tells us to "take up our cross daily and follow." The meaning was not lost on the first disciples, but it has been lost on many since. The cross was not and is not a fair piece of jewellery, but a cruel instrument of death. Bonhoeffer saw it correctly: The invitation of Jesus to us is an invitation to a funeral—our own. Herein is both the challenge and glory of life in Christ. Yes, I am summoned to die, but yes, I am promised life in all its fullness:

For whoever wants to save their life will lose it, but whoever loses their life for me will find it. (Matthew 16:25)

When we try to remake Jesus into a mascot, a guru, or a personal trainer, we lose Him. When we try to make Christ into someone who serves *our* agenda, we lose Christ. He is Lord and will make no bargains and cut no corners. The terms are not negotiable. The welcome invitation, "Come to me, all you who are weary and burdened, and I will give you rest" (Matthew 11:28) walks hand in hand with the command, "Anyone who loves their father or mother more than me is not worthy of me; anyone who loves their son or daughter more than me is not worthy of me" (Matthew 10:37).

Jesus aims to save us from sin and self and fit us for service and Heaven. My advice is that we let Him. You asked for a loving God, and you now have one. But His is not a soft love. It is not pink but red. His love is real, steady, and uncompromising. Lean into this following of Jesus. Don't hold back...it doesn't work (I've tried). It is when we get on with it and get into it (following) that we discover the all-sufficiency and sweetness of Jesus. There are not two Christs—an easy going one for easy going Christians, and a suffering, toiling one for exceptional believers. There is only one Christ.

Knowing this wonderful Jesus is worth leaving all else behind! He is the one who "knows" His sheep (John 10:27). He "gives them eternal life" (John 10:28). He promises that "they shall never perish" and that "no one can take them out of [His] hand" (John 10:28). He Himself is the prize. Yes, while following may be costly, not following will prove, in the long run, to be far more costly. While following will cost you all that you are, not following Christ will cost you *Him*.

Take heart. He gives us all the grace we need to follow. He lifts us when we fall. He promises to keep us "strong to the end" (1 Corinthians 1:8). *You* can be a faithful follower, because *He,* the Shepherd and Bishop of our souls, leads you.

****

He Leadeth Me

He leadeth me, O blessed thought!
O words with heav'nly comfort fraught!
Whate'er I do, where'er I be
Still 'tis God's hand that leadeth me.

He leadeth me, He leadeth me,
By His own hand He leadeth me;
His faithful foll'wer I would be,
For by His hand He leadeth me.

Sometimes 'mid scenes of deepest gloom,
Sometimes where Eden's bowers bloom,
By waters still, o'er troubled sea,
Still 'tis His hand that leadeth me.

Lord, I would place my hand in Thine,
Nor ever murmur nor repine;
Content, whatever lot I see,
Since 'tis my God that leadeth me.

And when my task on earth is done,
When by Thy grace the vict'ry's won,
E'en death's cold wave I will not flee,
Since God through Jordan leadeth me.
(Joseph Gilmore, 1901-2000)

Letter 4

Behold Your Sacrificial Substitute

All we like sheep have gone astray...and the Lord hath laid on him the iniquity of us all. Isaiah 53:6 (KJV)

Dear Ones,

One of the most important and influential books I ever read was John Stott's *The Cross of Christ*. The pages are falling out of my copy, for I have not only read and reread it, but I have used it over and over as a reference in sermon writing and personal devotion. I heartily recommend it! In his chapter entitled, "The Self-Substitution of God," Stott sums up the core of God's Gospel with these words: "For the essence of sin is man substituting himself for God, the essence of salvation is God substituting himself for man." This truth strikes at the heart of the Gospel.

Now, let's have some theological table-talk, just like we do when we are together.

The Gospel begins with bad news. Sobering, even offensive news: The test results are in and they are not good. The most offensive truth of Christianity (offensive that is, to the "natural" person), is that we, all of us, are sinners *by nature*. The doctrine of original sin tells us that the guilt and pollution of Adam (yes, I believe in a historical "Adam"), has been passed on to the whole human race. We "sin," therefore, because we are "sinners." This is the teaching of one of the most famous verses in the Bible, Romans 3:23:

> For all have sinned and fall short of the glory of God.

Diagnostically, this is a very telling verse. It helps us to understand the human predicament! The first thing we see in this telling verse is:

All have sinned.

The verb tense here is *aorist*. The aorist tense indicates a simple, past action. Hence, the Bible here is lumping the entire sin of the human race into one simple, past action, namely, the historical sin of Adam. At one time, the whole human race consisted of just two people (Adam and Eve), and they deliberately, wantonly, at a moment in time, simply rebelled against God. Thus, the whole race "sinned." The next thing we learn from Romans 3:23 is that the rest of us:

Fall short of the glory of God.

The tense here for "fall short" is the *"continuing present"* (or *present imperfect*). This refers to ongoing, continuous action. Yes, the human race *sinned* in Adam, but now it is *sinning* in us! We are doing a fine job of carrying on the family tradition of rebelling against God! When you read the account in Genesis 3, it becomes clear that Stott was right. The essence of sin was (is) man substituting himself for God:

For God knows that when you eat from it your eyes will be opened, and you will be like God, knowing good and evil. (Genesis 3:5)

Sin, whether Adam's passed on to us, or the choices we willingly and wrongly make, is our rebellious desire to be our own god. Even though the design of God is for us to be His vice-regents over the earth (an unimaginably noble calling), we refuse God's design, because we don't want to be accountable creatures. No, we want to be sovereign creators of our own destiny. This is why we are in such a mess!

But if sin is, at its essence, our substitution of ourselves for God, then salvation is, in essence, God substituting Himself in the person of Jesus Christ, His Son, for us. The Gospel is immeasurably glorious, and could never have been imagined by a human being. Just meditate upon the following sample of Bible verses which speak of this wondrous truth:

> God made him who had no sin to be sin for us, so that in him we might become the righteousness of God. (2 Corinthians 5:21)
>
> ...just as the Son of Man did not come to be served, but to serve, and to give his life as a ransom for many. (Matthew 20:28)
>
> "He himself bore our sins" in his body on the cross, so that we might die to sins and live for righteousness; "by his wounds you have been healed." (1 Peter 2:24)

I could give you so many more verses. I hope that you will search the Word for yourself. In it you will see everywhere, from the scapegoat in Leviticus 16, to the ram caught in the thicket in Genesis 22, to the very cross itself, that the Bible teaches that God Himself will supply the remedy for our sin, and that He has conclusively done just that in Christ on the cross.

The Bible teaches us that God the Father was "pleased to bruise Him [Jesus]" and to "make His soul an offering for sin" (Isaiah 53:10). By "pleased," the Bible does not intend that God the Father, in some sadistic sense, "enjoyed" seeing His Son die, but rather that His holy heart was satisfied as His righteousness was met in the sin-bearing substitution of Jesus Christ.

Wondrously, amazingly, this means that you do not have to bear your sin yourself. You and I have a *true* Saviour. Jesus is not just a good teacher (a good teacher is of little use to one caught in the thraldom of sin and guilt). He is not just a great leader (what good is a leader to one dead in trespasses?). Jesus is the "Lamb of God who takes away" our sin (John 1:29). Every religion stumbles over the sin issue. The Muslim hopes that his good deeds outweigh his bad. The Buddhist strives to extinguish all desire, for desire itself is sinful.

The Hindu seeks purification through millions of rebirths. But Jesus Christ invites us all to bring our sins to *Him*, and to trust Him to bear them Himself upon the cross.

Now, my dear children, it is vitally important that you actually *understand* this. The Bible tells us that Jesus was "set forth," by His Father as a "propitiation" (Romans 3:25, KJV). Now, you probably have not heard or used the word "propitiation" in a while (if ever). But it is a great Christian word! It means to "bear away wrath." It tells us that the righteous anger of a holy God was absorbed by Jesus Christ on the cross, so that it does not have to be borne by us. Christ was substituted for us, and He, being the infinitely valuable Son of God, with *one* offering of Himself, was able to pay for your sin, my sin, and the sins of all the world.

There is a beautiful moment in the Gospel of John where this glorious substitution is spotlighted. Go to chapter 18, the last night of Jesus' earthly life. The scene is Jesus before Pilate, and the crowd is choosing a rebel named Barabbas over Jesus. I wonder if John understood just what he was saying when he wrote these words:

Now Barabbas had taken part in a rebellion. (John 18:40)

The immediate reference was to a skirmish in which Barabbas the zealot had participated against the Romans. But there is a much deeper rebellion in which Barabbas had also taken part: Adam's. Barabbas was a willing participant in the mutinous rebellion of Adam. And so are you, and so am I. Take the word "Barabbas" out and put your own name there, as I have below:

Now John had taken part in a rebellion.

Who dies in this passage? Who lives? Who *deserved* to die? Who *deserved* to live? Jesus dies, Barabbas lives. Barabbas deserves to die, but walks. Jesus deserves to walk, but dies. The rebel is free, the obedient Saviour is condemned.

Substitution.

Oh how I hope that you will rejoice in the Gospel every day![8] Preach it to yourself, and then preach it to others! Live in the gracious stream of God's amazing grace and Gospel. Go to the Lord over and over with your guilt and shame, and *trust* in His finished work on the cross to be a full, sufficient, and perfect payment for your sins. There is no other balm for the wounded soul.

The main application here for the Christian is really very simple: **Believe the Gospel**. Visit John's Gospel, chapter 6 with me for a moment. Here is a remarkable scene where a delegation from large crowd asks Jesus a straightforward question:

> What must we do to do the works God requires?
> (John 6:28)

This is the question every religion in the world seeks to answer: "How can we please the 'gods' or God?" And the answers really are very much the same, regardless of the particular religion: Be a better person, fast, do penance, go on pilgrimage, deny your body of normal comforts, and so on. I am sure the delegation expected some such bundle of answers from Jesus, but they got nothing of the sort.

Jesus' answer was utterly disarming, and resulted in the delegation and the crowd turning and walking away:

> The work of God is this: to believe in the one he has sent. (John 6:29)

What a shocking answer to the religious enquirer! Certainly *we* must *do* something, but here is Jesus telling us to *believe* something, or more exactly, in someone—namely *Himself.* I think that we can fairly conclude that every religion on earth is somehow performance based. By this I mean, religions are about *people doing things to please God or the "gods."* In every religion, *people make promises to God or the "gods."* But in the Bible, God is the one who makes the promises. Do you see this? This is vital. He is the true and original Promise Keeper.

What we are called to do is *believe the promises*. In reality, every one of us is a Promise Breaker, or "miserable offender," to quote the Anglican prayer book. But we have a God who makes promises to sinners via the Gospel, and the "works God requires" is to *believe* those promises which are all in reference to His Son, Jesus Christ.

The crowd in John 6 could not handle this answer (v. 66). The Gospel undercuts every support to human pride and leaves the believer humbled before a holy God, with no boast except the wondrous mercy of God!

When I was a boy and right up through my teenage years, Billy Graham was often on television, preaching in one of his great crusades. My father and I always watched. I first heard the Gospel clearly from Billy Graham, right in our family room. I think he inspired me and taught me how to preach. Each and every word he spoke seemed chiselled out of granite and was delivered with the power of a jackhammer!

He closed every sermon with an invitation to "come to Christ," and as the choir began to sing "Just As I Am," thousands would stream forward to "receive Christ." So many times, I wanted to "go forward," kneel before the television, and give my life to Jesus, but alas, I was too embarrassed to do so in front of my own dear father, and then too afraid to live for Jesus amidst my teenage buddies. How God has had mercy upon me, to patiently endure my folly and fear of others and sovereignly save me!

Below is the great hymn "Just As I Am," by Charlotte Elliott.[9] How many have been blessed by this hymn! Just this week, in a gathering of precious Polish believers, I sang this hymn again, they in Polish, I in English:

****

Just As I Am

Just as I am, without one plea,
But that Thy blood was shed for me,
And that Thou bidst me come to Thee,
O Lamb of God, I come, I come.

Just as I am, and waiting not
To rid my soul of one dark blot,
To Thee whose blood can cleanse each spot,
O Lamb of God, I come, I come.

Just as I am, though tossed about
With many a conflict, many a doubt,
Fightings and fears within, without,
O Lamb of God, I come, I come.

Just as I am, poor, wretched, blind;
Sight, riches, healing of the mind,
Yea, all I need in Thee to find,
O Lamb of God, I come, I come.

Just as I am, Thou wilt receive,
Wilt welcome, pardon, cleanse, relieve;
Because Thy promise I believe,
O Lamb of God, I come, I come.

Just as I am, Thy love unknown
Hath broken every barrier down;
Now, to be Thine, yea, Thine alone,
O Lamb of God, I come, I come.
(Charlotte Elliott, 1789-1871)

Letter 5

Behold the Word Become Flesh

The Word became flesh and made his dwelling among us.
John 1:14

Dear Children,

Apollo 15 astronaut James Irwin, who stood on the surface of the moon, said that Jesus Christ walking on the earth is of more importance than man walking on the moon. Not only was he right, but the most significant event in history is without a doubt the coming of God to this troubled planet in the person of Jesus Christ. C.S. Lewis writes:

> The central miracle asserted by Christians is the Incarnation. They say that God became Man. Every other miracle prepares the way for this, or results from this.[10]

The Bible teaches us that God is one God who, somehow, is a "community" of three "persons." This is what we call the "Trinity." You and I will not figure this out! I'll give you Wayne Grudem's simple, one sentence definition, because I think it is the best summary of this amazing truth:

> God eternally exists as three persons, Father, Son, and Holy Spirit, and each person is fully God, and there is one God.[11]

You should be significantly amazed, a bit puzzled, somewhat disturbed, and genuinely intrigued right now. ("How can God be 'three persons' and 'one God' at the same time?") If you are not, then you have grown too used to Christian truth, and you need to ask God to put the "WOW!" back into your experience of Him. As Vance Havner said, "Plenty of church members are shaky about what they believe, while not many are shaken by what they believe."

Suffice it for now just to say that God is an eternal community of love and joy, and all true community we can ever experience exists only because of who God is in His very essence, the Trinity.

Now, let's get some childhood awe back and explore just a bit further: The Bible teaches us that one of the persons in this eternal community of love and joy, the one we know as Jesus, became a human being and walked on this earth. Our jaws should drop at the following Bible verse:

> And the Word was made flesh, and dwelt among us, (and we beheld his glory, the glory as of the only begotten of the Father,) full of grace and truth. (John 1:14, KJV)

So, when we encounter Jesus in the Bible (and we do, with the help of the Holy Spirit), we are encountering God...the Eternal God. The Apostle John tells us plainly that he and his fellow disciples beheld His glory when they walked, ate, slept, and talked with Jesus. Likewise, he wrote:

> That which was from the beginning, which we have heard, which we have seen with our eyes, which we have looked at and our hands have touched—this we proclaim concerning the Word of life. The life appeared; we have seen it and testify to it, and we proclaim to you the eternal life, which was with the Father and has appeared to us. (1 John 1:1-2)

I am concerned that we have grown too accustomed to this. The Incarnation, (that is, God becoming one of us in Jesus) should astound the Christian mind and heart. I want to invite you (plead with you if needed), to meditate upon just who Jesus is, to contemplate the profound claim of Christianity. Just feast upon the following few verses (though there are many more in the Bible):

> ...in these last days he has spoken to us by his Son, whom he appointed heir of all things, and through whom also he made the universe. The Son is the radiance of God's glory and the exact representation of his being, sustaining all things by his powerful word. (Hebrews 1:2, 3)

> Anyone who has seen me has seen the Father. (John 14:9)

> For to us a child is born, to us a son is given, and the government will be on his shoulders. And he will be called Wonderful Counselor, Mighty God, Everlasting Father, Prince of Peace. (Isaiah 9:6)

> For God was pleased to have all his fullness dwell in him. (Colossians 1:19)

> No one has ever seen God, but the one and only Son, who is himself God and is in closest relationship with the Father, has made him known. (John 1:18)

The world does not care if you vaguely believe in God. But Jesus challenges all such watery religion. To be a follower of Jesus is either the grossest idolatry, or the highest and purest purpose in life. To spend our lives promoting His fame in all the earth is either an utter waste of our lives, or the most meaningful use of them.

Dear ones, I firmly believe that the greatest battle that the Church of Jesus will face in the century ahead will be the battle to stay faithful to Jesus in regards to *who He is*. We are called to faithfulness to *Him* no matter what the cost may be. Our culture will not mind you believing in Jesus as long as you believe in a made-up Jesus. If you invent a Jesus that seems no different from Ghandi, or Krishna, or

Martin Luther King, Jr., no one will mind. If you follow a "private" Jesus, no one will care. But if you dare to follow, trust, and worship the real Jesus, you will be pitting yourself against a world which crucified Him...and it will crucify you.

It was Ravi Zacharias who rightly observed that these days, you can believe anything you want, just as long as you do not believe it is *true*. Today, it is fashionable to be foggy and vague. But we are called to be confident, not in ourselves, but in Jesus Christ.[12] We are called to be confident in *who He is*. This is what the Bible calls *faith*. Faith is confidence in Jesus. It is believing that what the Bible says about Jesus is true. The Bible is telling us that Jesus is the Son of God, God in the flesh, God with us, unique, and unequalled. No Mohammed, Buddha, or false god can stand beside Him, and all will one day bow before Him.

Will you live or die for this? I am asking you to. God is asking you to. This is Christianity: God became a man, "Immanuel, God with us," that He might be our rescuing Saviour.

I leave you today with my very dearest hymn. (I want this one at my funeral!) Take plenty of time over these words, let them nourish your soul:

****

My Song Is Love Unknown

My song is love unknown,
My Saviour's love to me;
Love to the loveless shown,
That they might lovely be.
O who am I, that for my sake
My Lord should take frail flesh and die?

He came from His blest throne
Salvation to bestow;
But men made strange, and none

The longed-for Christ would know:
But O! my Friend, my Friend indeed,
Who at my need His life did spend.

Sometimes they strew His way,
And His sweet praises sing;
Resounding all the day
Hosannas to their King:
Then "Crucify!" is all their breath,
And for His death they thirst and cry.

Why, what hath my Lord done?
What makes this rage and spite?
He made the lame to run,
He gave the blind their sight,
Sweet injuries! Yet they at these
Themselves displease, and 'gainst Him rise.

They rise and needs will have
My dear Lord made away;
A murderer they save,
The Prince of life they slay,
Yet cheerful He to suffering goes,
That He His foes from thence might free.

Here might I stay and sing,
No story so divine;
Never was love, dear King!
Never was grief like Thine.
This is my Friend, in Whose sweet praise
I all my days could gladly spend.
(Samuel Crossman, 1623-1683)

Letter 6

Behold Your Champion

But we do see Jesus, who was made lower than the angels for a little while, now crowned with glory and honor. Hebrews 2:9

Dear Ones,

The world loves champions. I love champions. I love to see someone compete and win. We idolize and immortalize winners. We build their statues, name our children after them, and create halls of fame in which we canonize them, preserving their accomplishments and memories.

There is one true Champion who puts all others in their rightful place: the sinner's place, the failure's place. For the reality is that our best fellows are failures, our heroes are flawed humans, our champions are chumps. Every person, left to himself, stands before a holy God not as a victor, but as a victim, one defeated by Satan and self, and in need of rescuing. The human condition, because of the mutiny of sin, is indeed a sad one. The best of us are fractured and weak, and but a moment away from catastrophe. (Just ask Lance Armstrong, Richard Nixon, King David, Marilyn Monroe, Kurt Cobain, and the list can go on and on.)

Recently, I walked through the Auschwitz death camp in Poland. What struck me so powerfully was not the thought, "this was something *they* did," but "this is something *we* do." That camp is a horrid testimony to the fallenness of our race, each and every one of us.

We humans are at the same time the most noble and the most tragic of all God's creation. We are both the crown and the gutter of the created order, but it was not this way at first. We were created in the very image of God! We are image-bearers of the Divine, stamped with the fingerprints of God Himself.

> You have made him for a little while lower than the angels;
> You have crowned him with glory and honor,
> And have appointed him over the works of Your hands. (Hebrews 2:7, 8, NASB)

We are the most like God of anything in all of creation. But because of our mutiny, we are also the most like Satan. The human predicament is profound. The original design was for us to rule as God's vice-regents over the earth: "You have appointed him over the works of Your hands." God ordained it this way. Hebrews 2:8 (NASB) goes on to say, in reference to mankind:

> For in subjecting all things to him, He left nothing that is not subject to him.

Ruling is part of what it means to be an image-bearer. But sin and rebellion messed it all up, the would-be ruler became the slave, and creation became subject to the frustration of thorns and weeds, pain, and sweat. Again, Hebrews 2:8 (NASB) says:

> But now we do not yet see all things subjected to him.

That is the understatement of all time. All things are certainly not "subjected to" us. We are not exercising godlike dominion, and whenever we do exercise some form of dominion, we usually pollute and wreck things. When we look to man and what we are and do; things can look pretty bleak. I read an article recently that said we are trashing up space! There is too much old junk orbiting the earth and scientists don't know what to do with it. We have even left our stuff on the moon, and now on Mars. I understand there is talk now of colonizing Mars by 2025. This is fine, but we will need missionaries and a church there, because Mars will now have sinners living on it. Clearly, everywhere we mutinous rebels go, we spread trash, pain, death, disease, and destruction there. Pity the universe!

If our lives were portrayed in an old style Western, we would *all* be wearing black hats! But! There is *one* good man in this universe. There is *one* man who wears a white hat. There is *one* who does rule. When He walked on this sad planet, he ruled the wind and waves, sickness and death, Satan and sin. We do not have to look at Him and cringe. He is the only *normal* person to have ever lived. He has nothing for which to apologize. Of Him, we can be proud. Hebrews 2:8,9 says:

> In putting everything under them (that is, we humans), God left nothing that is not subject to them. Yet at present we do not see everything subject to them. *But we do see Jesus, who was made lower than the angels for a little while, now crowned with glory and honor...*

Jesus was "made a little lower than the angels." That is, He became one of us. But look at Him now: "crowned with glory and honor." Finally, a good guy! At last, there is someone who is not covered in shame! Finally, a CHAMPION. Finally someone who does not have a closet full of skeletons, who will not be found to be a fraud; the real deal. Our Jesus has gone before us and has defeated evil. Tempted in all ways like us, He never sinned. We have a friend, a victorious friend, in high places! We despair much when we look at ourselves, we despair not when we look at Him. As the cross loomed large before Him, Jesus declared: "now the prince of this world will be driven out" (John 12:31). Even when Jesus Christ was in His weakest hour, in His crucifixion, He was triumphing over Satan (see Colossians 2:15). He is victorious, and He is *our* Shepherd, Brother, Friend, Lord, Saviour, Bishop, and Advocate. He has been tried and tempted and has emerged faultless. He has stared death in the face, allowed it to give Him its worst, and has come forth in victory. He has absorbed the righteous wrath of His Holy Father, a wrath which we deserved, and has been vindicated through His resurrection.

Go deep with this. Think on it, sing about it, pray it into your heart, mind, and experience.

This should give us great encouragement. One old-time Puritan put it this way: "If the head is through the hedge, the body is sure to follow." Likewise, if the head is above the waves, the body will not drown, though it be swamped. If we are united to Christ by faith, then we are sure to share in His victory. If Christ has triumphed over Satan, sin, and death, then we shall triumph (have triumphed!) with Him. Just feast upon the following verses:

> No, in all these things (the severest trials) we are more than conquerors through him who loved us. (Romans 8:37)

> For I have come down from heaven not to do my will but to do the will of him who sent me. And this is the will of him who sent me, that I shall lose none of all that he has given me, but raise them up at the last day. (John 6:38, 39)

> Christ Jesus, who has destroyed death and has brought life and immortality to light through the gospel. (2 Timothy 1:10)

> Because I live, you also will live. (John 14:19)

> When you were dead in your sins and in the uncircumcision of your flesh, God made you alive with Christ. He forgave us all our sins, having canceled the charge of our legal indebtedness, which stood against us and condemned us; he has taken it away, nailing it to the cross. And having disarmed the powers and authorities, he made a public spectacle of them, triumphing over them by the cross. (Colossians 2:13-15)

We can either focus upon ourselves, our failures, our weaknesses (and yes, certainly, there is a need and right time to bemoan our sins and frailties), or we can rivet our attention on Christ and His victory, and our victory in Him. For the Bible teaches us that we are:

Crucified with Christ (Galatians 2:20)

Dead to sin and buried with Christ (Romans 6:3)

Alive with Christ (Ephesians 2:5)

Risen with Christ (Romans 6:5)

Seated with Christ in Heaven (Ephesians 2:6)

More than conquerors in Christ (Romans 8:37)

Future rulers with Christ (2 Timothy 2:12)

These are transformational, liberating truths. Being faithful means that we take these truths and *apply* them to our lives, believe *them* and say no to the lies that we have believed; lies which have held us in bondage.

We honour God when we believe what He says about us; both in the positive and the negative. The Puritan, John Owen, said that the two most difficult things for a pastor to do are: 1) Get people to believe what God says about them in regard to their deep sinfulness in Adam, and; 2) Get people to believe what God says about them in regard to their glorious salvation in Christ. We honour God as being truthful and faithful when we believe, even with great anguish, His terrible diagnosis of us: Dead in Adam, in sin and transgression, and without hope. And we honour God as being truthful and faithful when we believe, even with great thankfulness and joy, His declaration regarding us: Alive in Christ and overwhelmingly victorious in Him.

Behold Jesus, your Champion. Rejoice in His victory over sin, death, and Satan. Boast of Him. Crown Him as your Captain. Walk in His victory. Celebrate His triumphant life, death, and resurrection. The Church used to sing hymns of battle and victory in Jesus. We don't do much of this these days. We have grown too soft, too timid. We could easily truncate Paul's declaration, "We wrestle not against flesh and blood," to simply "We wrestle not!" But wrestle and fight we must! And we can do so in sure hope of victory because Jesus has already triumphed.

Here is a hymn that we used to sing all through the hills and valleys of Cornwall. How many truly great, Christ-exalting meetings we had in those days! These stirring words of Charles Wesley simply cannot be surpassed in their recognition of Jesus as our Champion:

****

Jesus the Name High Over All

Jesus, the name high over all,
In hell, or earth, or sky:
Angels and men before it fall,
And devils fear and fly.

Jesus, the name to sinners dear,
The name to sinners giv'n;
It scatters all their guilty fear,
It brings them peace of heav'n.

Jesus the prisoner's fetters breaks,
And bruises Satan's head;
Pow'r into strengthless souls He speaks,
And life into the dead.

Oh, that the world might taste and see,
The riches of His grace!
The arms of love that compass me,
Would all mankind embrace.

Him as my righteousness I show,
His saving truth proclaim:
'Tis all my business here below,
To cry, Behold the Lamb!

Happy, if with my latest breath
I may but gasp His name:
Preach Him to all, and cry in death,
"Behold, behold the Lamb!"
(Charles Wesley, 1707-1788)

Letter 7

Behold the Father's Final Word

In the past God spoke to our ancestors through the prophets at many times and in various ways, but in these last days he has spoken to us by his Son. Hebrews 1:1, 2

Dear Ones,

One of the key battles of my life has been to see a people convinced that God has spoken authoritatively and sufficiently in Jesus Christ. What I mean is this: The Bible teaches that God's Son, Jesus, "the Word made flesh," is God's full and final word to the human race. By this, I do not mean that God is now silent, but I do mean that God has revealed His saving purposes fully in Jesus. There is no other "prophet" (i.e. Mohammed, Joseph Smith, Charles Russell, Mary Baker Eddy, Rev. Moon, etc.) who comes with more revelation for us about God and the way of salvation.

Now, I do not for one minute think that any of you are going to go off into some cult! But I am concerned that many who name Christ as their Lord and Saviour, and claim to believe that the Bible is God's definitive case for His Son, in reality, spend little time seeking Him in His Word. Many rarely satisfy their souls in the Scriptures, and run endlessly here and there, wanting some "word" from God that some-one else has gotten for them while they have been spiritually lazy.

You know I believe that God rests His case for His Son with the testimony of Christ written in the pages of the Bible. You also know that I believe I actually meet with Jesus when I open the Word, lift my heart to Heaven, ask the Holy Spirit to help me, and *read the Bible*. My soul is nourished, my mind is instructed, my life is directed. I would rather read the Gospels than see an angel, or have a vision, or have someone give me what they believe to be a word from the Lord for me. I am not saying that there is no value in any of these things, but I am saying that when I encounter Jesus in the Bible, I am encountering the Word from the Father to me, and nothing else can compare with that.

My friend, Dietrich Bonhoeffer (I know him through his writings and will one day, I am sure, know him face to face), says:

> But to deviate from the truth for the sake of some prospect of hope of our own can never be wise, however slight that deviation might be. It is not our judgement of the situation which can show us what is wise, but only the truth of the Word of God. Here alone lies the promise of God's faithfulness and help. It will always be true that the wisest course for the disciple is always to abide solely by the Word of God in all simplicity.[13]

Now, this might not be exciting enough for some. But be wary, dear children, of anyone who claims to have *immediate* access to God. God *mediates* Himself to us through Christ, via the Scriptures, in the inspiration of the Holy Spirit. This keeps us from losing our way and doing immeasurable damage to ourselves and others. Watch out for the one who closes his Bible, but still claims to be speaking out God's heart. Every great and true revival in Christian history has kept the Bible at its centre. Moreover, the power of God was never lacking in those great times of refreshing! Charles Wesley, who saw firsthand the power of a Bible-centred revival, testified in verse that:

> He speaks; and, listening to His voice,
> New life the dead receive,
> The mournful, broken hearts rejoice,
> The humble poor believe.[14]

"But," you may say, "Dad, how can you limit God to the Bible? Certainly God cannot be confined to a book!" My reply would be, "True, *we* cannot limit God, but *God* can limit us! He can limit us to the Bible and say, 'My final, full Word to the human race is embodied in my Son, Jesus, and faithfully recorded in the Bible. Stick with Him and my Word, and you will truly begin to know me, prosper in your soul and life, and will be a great blessing to others as I use you mightily.'"

Now I know that we all want to hear God speak. How wonderful it is that God is not mute! How amazing that He condescends to make Himself known, that He is a gracious God who reveals Himself! But here is my word of caution to you all, and I pray that you will hear me out:

Yes, I believe that God can speak directly into our lives, through a "word of knowledge," an impression, a dream, and so on. But I fear that we can very easily become too reliant upon such, even spiritually lazy, in a sense asking the Holy Spirit to work overtime. We can also easily be misled by these, for we often forget that the remnants of sin are still deeply hidden in our hearts, and we are all susceptible to self-deception.[15] To not be willing to do the basic, sometimes difficult "work" of reading God's Word, seeking Him in the Bible, ever discovering who He is and what His heart for us is, but then *expecting* Him to speak through some other means (which He may do in His graciousness), is presumptuous on our part. It is also rude and ungrateful, for it fails to honour the incredible grace of God for becoming the Word made flesh and ensuring that the written Word be provided for us.

Take a moment and consider these words from Martin Luther:

> For some years now, I have read through the Bible twice every year. If you picture the Bible to be a mighty tree and every word   a little branch, I have shaken every one of these branches because I wanted to know what it was and what it meant...Nothing is more effectual against the devil, the world, the flesh, and all evil thoughts than to occupy oneself with the Word of God, talk about it and meditate on it.[16]

If you want to prosper over the length of your life, truly growing in your walk with God, then believe with me (and millions of others through the ages!) that Jesus is the finished Word, and that the Bible is God's clear, authoritative, inspired, sufficient communication of His saving grace towards us. Learn to meet God in the Bible. Learn of His ways, character, heart, and sovereignty. Be ever grateful for Jesus, the Word made flesh, and the Bible, which faithfully gives Him to us. As you seek Jesus with your heart open to Heaven and the Bible open before you, you will be preserved from a thousand errors and nourished to the depths of your soul.

Let me give you one more picture to help you understand just what I mean. Fire belongs in the fireplace, and not in the chimney. We need fire in our hearts, combined with cool heads. Passion needs to marry precision. A burning love for Jesus (which I *certainly* want) needs to be embraced by a considered apprehension of solid Bible knowledge. John Wesley put it this way:

> Let us unite the two, so long divided: Knowledge (that is, sound biblical theology), and Vital Piety (true experience of Jesus).

Oh how the Scriptures give us a *big* vision of our *great* God! When you receive Jesus as the final revelation of truth, and the Bible as a full and sufficient repository of Jesus, this truth, your soul begins to soar as on eagle's wings. Here is a hymn which will lift you on the rising currents of truth to the heights of worship. (The author, you will see, lived to the ripe old age of *30.* Vance Havner wisely wrote, "Life is not measured by length but by depth. Birthdays tell us how long we have been on the road, not how far we have travelled.") It reminds us that good theology and true worship are friends which must always be found together:

****

Praise to the Lord, the Almighty, the King of Creation

Praise to the Lord, the Almighty, the King of creation!
O my soul, praise Him, for He is thy health and salvation!
All ye who hear, now to His temple draw near;
Praise Him in glad adoration.

Praise to the Lord, who over all things so wondrously reigneth,
Shelters thee under His wings, yea, so gently sustaineth!
Hast thou not seen how thy desires ever have been
Granted in what He ordaineth?

Praise to the Lord, who hath fearfully, wondrously, made thee;
Health hath vouchsafed and, when heedlessly falling, hath stayed thee.
What need or grief ever hath failed of relief?
Wings of His mercy did shade thee.

Praise to the Lord, who doth prosper thy work and defend thee;
Surely His goodness and mercy here daily attend thee.
Ponder anew what the Almighty can do,
If with His love He befriend thee.

Praise to the Lord, who, when tempests their warfare are waging,
Who, when the elements madly around thee are raging,
Biddeth them cease, turneth their fury to peace,
Whirlwinds and waters assuaging.

Praise to the Lord, who, when darkness of sin is abounding,
Who, when the godless do triumph, all virtue confounding,
Sheddeth His light, chaseth the horrors of night,
Saints with His mercy surrounding.

Praise to the Lord, O let all that is in me adore Him!

All that hath life and breath, come now with praises before Him.

Let the Amen sound from His people again,

Gladly for aye we adore Him.

(Joachim Neander, 1650-1680)

Letter 8

Behold the One Who Is Full of Grace and Truth

And the Word was made flesh, and dwelt among us, (and we beheld His glory, the glory as of the only begotten of the Father,) full of grace and truth. John 1:14 (KJV)

My Dear Children,

"This man welcomes sinners, and eats with them!" (Luke 15:2). So said the Pharisees and teachers of the law, certain that they were casting aspersions upon Jesus. What kind of a rabbi would attract such a crowd as this: tax collectors, prostitutes, political troublemakers? No average rabbi would! But Jesus was not your average, "off the peg" rabbi. Jesus was and is the friend of sinners. How thankful I am that Jesus welcomes sinners, for now there is hope for you and me. If Jesus were the "good person's" God, I would have no hope. But Jesus is the "bad person's" God!

Hear Him:

> *It is* not those who are healthy who need a physician, but those who are sick; I did not come to call the righteous, but sinners.
> (Mark 2:17, NASB)

Is there a doctor in the house? Yes, Dr. Jesus. Is there a help for the wounded soul? Yes. Is there a friend for the sinner? Most assuredly. Dear ones, this is what is so wonderfully different about Jesus Christ. Every "religion" somehow is about "measuring up." Christianity is about finding and taking the sinners' place before the cross. Wonderfully, remarkably, it is there that you find Jesus Christ Himself kneeling beside you, welcoming you, assuring you that He has been waiting for you with a heart of grace, ready to forgive and restore.

I cannot measure up. I have tried and tried. But Jesus only asks me to recognize my *need*, to confess my *mutiny and rebellion,* and then to take the *low place*, the place of *receiving*.

The Bible teaches us that Jesus Christ is "full of grace and truth" (John 1:14). I just want to unpack this beautiful verse with you for a few minutes:

First, Jesus is *full* of something. The Greek word here is *pleres*, which means *abounding* or *abundant*. We get the words *plenary* and *plenty* from the same root. There is no shortage of this something in Jesus. There is no looming crisis that might cause demand to outstrip supply.

Next, Jesus is full of *grace*. The word here is *charis*. It means *favour, acceptance, a kindness done without expectation of return*. It speaks of the absolute freeness of the love of God towards us, and by definition, insists that *we are undeserving*. Jesus Christ is *full* of this!

Finally, Jesus is full of *truth*. The Greek word here is *aletheia*. It literally means that the unseen reality of a thing agrees with the seen appearance. In terms of Jesus Christ being "full of...truth," the meaning here is, where Jesus is concerned, what you see is what you get—fully, and in every aspect. The word can fairly be translated *faithfulness* or *truthfulness*.

So, we could translate this powerful little verse like this:

> Jesus Christ has, without shortage or limit, an abundance of kindness and favour—giving love for us. He does not need to or ever expect to get anything back. This is not just a surface thing with Jesus, it is what He is really like—way down deep—and He will never be any other way.

Because Jesus is "full of grace and truth," Heaven is going to be full of surprises. We cannot gain Heaven by religious efforts, and we cannot lose Heaven by our failures. Eternal life is a gift which we receive. I am telling you, *no one, nowhere, at any time* could have ever thought up the glorious Gospel. It runs so counterintuitively to the way we think. We naturally operate, without fail, on the basis of getting what we deserve, but the Gospel is fuelled by the grace and truth that is in God alone. In Heaven, we will be shocked by: 1) Who is *not* there, and; 2) Who *is* there. To the religious leaders of His day who thought of salvation being something deserved, Jesus said:

> Truly I say to you that the tax collectors and prostitutes will get into the kingdom of God before you. (Matthew 21:31, NASB)

Every hopeless, ruined sinner who has fled to Jesus for mercy, to find Him "full of grace and truth," will exist in eternity as Exhibit A of the wonders of the God who saves sinners, bearing timeless testimony to the limitless depth and breadth of God's grace, made available through Jesus Christ. Get ready for some glorious surprises! I am wondering if Oscar Wilde (1854-1900) just might be there. What a torbid mess he was![17] Totally given over to sensuality, this brilliant man died tragically young in Paris. In 1895, he was convicted of gross indecency (homosexual practices) and sentenced to two years hard labour. Through this experience, he wrote *The Ballad of Reading Gaol*. Though a long and tortuous poem, I think there may be a testimony of brokenness and conversion within it. Look at the stanza below:

> Ah! happy they whose hearts can break
>> And peace of pardon win!
> How else may man make straight his plan
>> And cleanse his soul from Sin?
> How else but through a broken heart
>> May Lord Christ enter in?

Ravi Zacharias tells us that upon his deathbed, Wilde asked his onetime lover, Robbie Ross, the remorse-filled question: "Robbie, all those boys we had, did you ever love one of them for their self?"

"No, not one," replied Robbie.

"Nor me," said Wilde. "Now get me a priest, for this is now my only hope."[18]

It would not surprise me one bit to one day find Wilde dressed in white, praising God and the Lamb before His throne for His saving grace and mercy. How tragic that he wasted his years on earth, but how wondrous is the Lord Jesus towards us sinners. Trophies of grace we are, every one of us.

Oh, that you will make much of Jesus and His grace! Begin with yourself. Believe the Gospel for yourself first. Preach it to yourself every day. Trust Christ to cover your sins and to clothe you with His righteousness. But then, oh yes, make much of Jesus to others. How this world of ruined sinners needs Him who is "full of grace and truth!" How many Oscar Wildes are out there, prodigals a long way from the Father, prime candidates for Him who is "full of grace and truth!"

Charles Wesley was a sinner, but not of the Wilde type. The son of a vicar, he was trapped in the self-righteousness that religion offers. Though he was an ordained priest in the Church of England, he was thus as ripe for Hell and in as much need of grace as Oscar Wilde, or you...or I. On May 21, 1738, while in bed recovering from a bout with pneumonia that had nearly killed him, Wesley came to a place of surrender and trust in Jesus, the sinners' friend.[19] Below is a great hymn, thought to be written as a testimony to his conversion. Make it the hymn of your heart too!

****

And Can it Be?

And can it be that I should gain
An interest in the Savior's blood?
Died He for me, who caused His pain—
For me, who Him to death pursued?

Amazing love! How can it be,
That Thou, my God, shouldst die for me?
Amazing love! How can it be,
That Thou, my God, shouldst die for me?

'Tis mystery all: th'Immortal dies:
Who can explore His strange design?
In vain the firstborn seraph tries
To sound the depths of love divine.
'Tis mercy all! Let earth adore,
Let angel minds inquire no more.
'Tis mercy all! Let earth adore;
Let angel minds inquire no more.

He left His Father's throne above
So free, so infinite His grace—
Emptied Himself of all but love,
And bled for Adam's helpless race:
'Tis mercy all, immense and free,
For O my God, it found out me!
'Tis mercy all, immense and free,
For O my God, it found out me!

Long my imprisoned spirit lay,
Fast bound in sin and nature's night;
Thine eye diffused a quickening ray—
I woke, the dungeon flamed with light;
My chains fell off, my heart was free,
I rose, went forth, and followed Thee.
My chains fell off, my heart was free,
I rose, went forth, and followed Thee.

Still the small inward voice I hear,

That whispers all my sins forgiven;

Still the atoning blood is near,

That quenched the wrath of hostile Heaven.

I feel the life His wounds impart;

I feel the Savior in my heart.

I feel the life His wounds impart;

I feel the Savior in my heart.

No condemnation now I dread;

Jesus, and all in Him, is mine;

Alive in Him, my living Head,

And clothed in righteousness divine,

Bold I approach th'eternal throne,

And claim the crown, through Christ my own.

Bold I approach th'eternal throne,

And claim the crown, through Christ my own.

(Charles Wesley, 1707-1788)

Letter 9

Behold Your Magnificent King

And they sang the song of Moses, the bond-servant of God, and the song of the Lamb, saying,

> *"Great and marvelous are Your works,*
> *O Lord God, the Almighty;*
> *Righteous and true are Your ways,*
> *King of the nations!"* Revelation 15:3 (NASB)

Dear Children,

In C.S. Lewis' *Prince Caspian: The Return to Narnia*, Lucy encounters Aslan, the lion king, her hero and champion, once again:

> "Aslan, Aslan. Dear Aslan," sobbed Lucy. "At last."
>
> The great beast rolled over on his side so that Lucy fell, half sitting and half lying between his front paws. He bent forward and just touched her nose with his tongue. His warm breath came all round her. She gazed up into the large wise face.
>
> "Welcome, child," he said.
>
> "Aslan," said Lucy, "you're bigger."
>
> "That is because you are older, little one," answered he.
>
> "Not because you are?"
>
> "I am not. But every year you grow, you will find me bigger."[20]

Remembering that Aslan is a picture of Jesus Christ, Lucy's observation of him is glorious. (C.S. Lewis was a genius!)

Remember when you were a kid, and everything was "big"? Your bedroom looms huge in your memory, as does your tree house, school, until you return to those old haunts and marvel at how small they have all become! In reality, *they* have not changed, *you* have. You have grown, and the things which once appeared so large to your eye have gained their proper perspective. Dickens' grown-up David Copperfield, in reference to his boyhood home, recalls:

> Here is a long passage-what enormous perspective I make of it-leading from Peggotty's kitchen to the front door...

Everything in life is that way (almost everything, as we shall see). Things we once saw as so big, valuable, and magnificent grow smaller and lose significance as life goes by. Medals tarnish and crowns corrode. Today's winters are not so glorious and snowy, the summers not so warm and carefree, the strawberries not so juicy and sweet, as our memories have made yesterday's.

The importance of "stuff" shrinks with time. This is what makes Aslan unique. Lucy encounters him, but not as he was. Unlike the bedroom he is not in reality smaller than remembered. "Aslan," said Lucy, "you're bigger." In fact, Aslan has not grown, but as Lucy has, she now sees Aslan more truly as he is...and he is BIGGER than she first thought.

> But every year you grow, you will find me bigger.

So it is with our King, Jesus. Because He is who He is (the Eternal Son of God), He is not in the process of becoming something greater or bigger. He is eternally perfect. However, as we grow in our Christian walk and mature in our faith, far from Him shrinking in our eyes, we esteem Him more fully. He is magnified before us, ever more wonderful, ever more powerful, ever more worthy of praise, ever more glorious, ever more able...BIGGER.

Our King, Jesus, does not disappoint. He is not like the gift which looks so amazing in the catalogue, but when opened upon delivery, is actually half the expected size. True, the Big Mac that comes out of the box never looks as good as the Big Mac on the menu, but Jesus, as wonderful as He appears in the Bible, is even more wonderful when experienced and encountered, now through the eyes of faith, then face to face.

Dear ones, you and I are just *beginning* this journey of discovery with Jesus Christ. Thus far, whatever we have truly experienced of Him is certain to grow in our estimation as we continue with Him...even into eternity. With Jesus, each day grows better than the one before, the "new" never wears off. There is always another adventure with Him, a new truth to delve into, explore, and glory in—a yet undiscovered facet of His character in which to rejoice.

The Jesus of the Bible is worthy of our absolute surrender, our highest thoughts, our noblest efforts, our purest adoration, our greatest enjoyments, and our costliest sacrifices.

Just to help you gain a yet "bigger" apprehension of our King Jesus, see the great Isaac Watts hymn below, "Jesus Shall Reign Where'er the Sun." I have included all fourteen verses! Take some time with this great hymn and let your King be magnified in your eyes:

****

Jesus Shall Reign Where'er The Sun

Jesus shall reign where'er the sun
Does his successive journeys run;
His kingdom stretch from shore to shore,
Till moons shall wax and wane no more.

Behold the islands with their kings,
And Europe her best tribute brings;
From north to south the princes meet,
To pay their homage at His feet.

There Persia, glorious to behold,
There India shines in eastern gold;
And barb'rous nations at His word
Submit, and bow, and own their Lord.

To Him shall endless prayer be made,
And praises throng to crown His head;
His Name like sweet perfume shall rise
With every morning sacrifice.

People and realms of every tongue
Dwell on His love with sweetest song;
And infant voices shall proclaim
Their early blessings on His Name.

Blessings abound wherever He reigns;
The prisoner leaps to lose his chains;
The weary find eternal rest,
And all the sons of want are blessed.

Where He displays His healing power,
Death and the curse are known no more:
In Him the tribes of Adam boast
More blessings than their father lost.

Let every creature rise and bring
Peculiar honors to our King;
Angels descend with songs again,
And earth repeat the loud amen!

Great God, whose universal sway
The known and unknown worlds obey,

Now give the kingdom to Thy Son,
Extend His power, exalt His throne.

The scepter well becomes His hands;
All Heav'n submits to His commands;
His justice shall avenge the poor,
And pride and rage prevail no more.

With power He vindicates the just,
And treads th'oppressor in the dust:
His worship and His fear shall last
Till hours, and years, and time be past.

As rain on meadows newly mown,
So shall He send his influence down:
His grace on fainting souls distills,
Like heav'nly dew on thirsty hills.

The heathen lands, that lie beneath
The shades of overspreading death,
Revive at His first dawning light;
And deserts blossom at the sight.

The saints shall flourish in His days,
Dressed in the robes of joy and praise;
Peace, like a river, from His throne
Shall flow to nations yet unknown.
(Isaac Watts, 1674-1748)

Letter 10

Behold Your Judge

For we must all appear before the judgment seat of Christ.
2 Corinthians 5:10

Dear Children,

If you will live well, you must live every day in the truth that you will one day give an account to God. Do not make the dangerous (and wrong) assumption that our gracious God is in any sense a pushover. The dark background upon which the diamond of the Gospel shines is the reality that God is a holy God who hates sin. He has a just, righteous, and deserved wrath towards all sin and evil, whatever the guise.[21]

We need to understand that God does not save us because we are cute, cuddly, and irresistible. He does not save us because *we* are wonderful. He saves us because *He* is wonderful. He saves us as a display of His glory, demonstrating that He is the God who says, "I will have mercy on whom I will have mercy, and...compassion on whom I will have compassion" (Exodus 33:19). I cannot overemphasize this.

You will never understand the Gospel, nor truly praise, worship, and joyfully serve the Lord until you understand that it is about God's goodness, not yours. You are bad, and God saves you because He is good. Yes, it is true, you and I are valuable, because we are bearers of God's image, but even this truth serves to make our sinfulness that much more heinous and damnable. God does not judge horses and pigeons, for they are not His image-bearers. Humans are the moral rebels, deserving of wrath, yet humans are those upon whom God bestows salvation. God saves us because He is astounding in His mercy. His grace shines so brightly, because it is displayed against the backdrop of deserved judgment. *Get this, and you begin to understand the wondrous Gospel.*

I know that on that great day of judgment when the thoughts, motives, actions of all are laid bare before Jesus Christ, I will stand as one justified by grace through faith, whose sin has been borne by Jesus Himself, and in whose righteousness I am now and will be then clothed. This is the wonder of the Gospel. This is what it means to be justified by the grace of God. Jesus, the Son of God, has promised His Father that He "shall lose none of all that he has given me, but raise them up at the last day" (John 6:39). This is like being told today that you are guaranteed an A+ on your final exam. The verdict of that day is rendered *now*.

But wait a minute! Does this mean that all we have to do is loaf it into Heaven? Is our Christian life to be one of hot tub ease as we bubble our way into the lap of Jesus? What of the many New Testament commands and encouragements to wrestle, fight, run, watch, battle, contend, and be diligent? What about the warnings against cherishing sin, continuing in evil, slumbering, loving the world?

I do not want to squander the grace of God! The balance comes as we realize that God's grace does not grant us a license to laziness, but power for godliness. It reminds me continually that I, a saved and safe child of God, will have to give an account to my Lord. My life will be weighed before a holy God. Saved though I am, *because* I am saved, I want to be able to give a faithful account, one that honours the grace which has been lavishly bestowed upon me day after day. Jesus speaks of rewards for us in eternity.[22] To be sure, we are not saved by works in any way, but if the Lord tells us of eternal rewards (which I am sure have to do with our capacity to know and enjoy Christ in Heaven), then who am I to argue with Him?[23]

We will *all* give an account of ourselves to God (Romans 14:12). There is a sense in which being born again increases the responsibility to give a *good* account on that great day of judgment. God the Father has entrusted and appointed His Son to be the judge of all (Acts 10:42).

Those who have rejected Christ, ignored Him, scoffed at Him, or denied Him will one day stand before Him. How great is Jesus Christ! What a sobering truth! Jesus Christ stands at the end of history and *no one* will be able to avoid Him, send an attorney, priest, wife, or friend to represent him. All of us, the great and small, princes, presidents, peasants and paupers, will stand before Jesus Christ and be judged:

> Then I saw a great white throne and him who was seated on it. The earth and the heavens fled from his presence, and there was no place for them. And I saw the dead, great and small, standing before the throne, and books were opened. Another book was opened, which is *the book* of life. The dead were judged according to what they had done as recorded in the books. The sea gave up the dead that were in it, and death and Hades gave up the dead that were in them, and *each person* was judged according to what they had done. (Revelation 20:11-13)

Children, I say again, "What you think about when you think about Jesus is the most important thing about you." How desperately true this is! How we need to entertain true, biblical notions of Christ and do away with idolatrous notions of Him which we have fashioned after our own imaginations...little "Jesuses" not worthy of the name nor the title, "Lord"! An anaemic Christ will lead to an anaemic disciple. We need to behold Jesus not just as our friend and brother, for He is, but also as our Lord and Judge, as He also is. The day will come when "every eye shall see Him" (Revelation 1:7), and for many that will not be a good day. People flippantly say, "When I get upstairs, I've got a bone or two to pick with Jesus." I seriously doubt they will get around to it:

> Then the kings of the earth and the great men and the commanders and the rich and the strong and every slave and free man hid themselves in the caves and among the rocks of the mountains; and they said to the mountains and to the rocks, "Fall on us and hide us from the presence of Him who sits on the throne, and from the wrath of the

Lamb; for the great day of their wrath has come, and who is able to stand?" (Revelation 6:15-17, NASB)

I think most of us who name the name of Jesus as our Lord need a good dose of reverence. Perhaps the lost will begin to fear Christ when we do! Psalm 2:11 gets it right:

Rejoice with trembling.

Loved ones, if you would live well today, you must live with that great day in view. Never lose sight that you will give an account to Jesus Christ. Never forget that there are consequences of eternal significance which are being determined *right now*—by your decisions today. It is my prayer that you will one day be able to say what the Apostle Paul was able to say as his earthly pilgrimage was drawing to its close:

For I am already being poured out as a drink offering, and the time of my departure has come. I have fought the good fight, I have finished the course, I have kept the faith; in the future there is laid up for me the crown of righteousness, which the Lord, the righteous Judge, will award to me on that day; and not only to me, but also to all who have loved His appearing. (2 Timothy 4:6-8, NASB)

I leave you with another Isaac Watts hymn. As you meditate upon it, weigh your life in the light of eternity.

****

Am I a Soldier of the Cross?

Am I a soldier of the cross,
A follower of the Lamb,
And shall I fear to own His cause,
Or blush to speak His Name?

Must I be carried to the skies
On flowery beds of ease,
While others fought to win the prize,
And sailed through bloody seas?

Are there no foes for me to face?
Must I not stem the flood?
Is this vile world a friend to grace,
To help me on to God?

Sure I must fight if I would reign;
Increase my courage, Lord.
I'll bear the toil, endure the pain,
Supported by Thy Word.

Thy saints in all this glorious war
Shall conquer, though they die;
They see the triumph from afar,
By faith's discerning eye.

When that illustrious day shall rise,
And all Thy armies shine
In robes of victory through the skies,
The glory shall be Thine.
(Isaac Watts, 1674-1748)

Letter 11

Behold the One Whose Love Is Better Than Life

Because your love is better than life, my lips will glorify you.
Psalm 63:3

Dearest Family,

I can clearly remember being at Anfield Stadium in Liverpool, 1984. Billy Graham was preaching a sermon on Hezekiah. He began that message in front of 50,000 people with these words: "Some people live too long." Those words struck right at my heart. We are programmed to value life in terms of *duration* more than in terms of *donation*. But could it be that we treasure this life too much? Could it be that our souls are suffering because we have misplaced our affection? Could it be that knowing Jesus Christ and His love is actually better than life as we know it? When the Apostle Paul said, "I desire to depart and be with Christ, which is *better by far*" (Philippians 1:23), were these the sentiments of a "super Christian" or "religious wacko," or was he expressing a heart longing for Jesus which should be normal for every one of us?

Now this life can have some very precious moments: births, marriages, family gatherings, warm friendships, and more. How many precious times we have when we gather around our table and feast! Christians are rarely called to asceticism. Being morbid is not the same thing as being godly. Yes, there are days of fasting and weeping, and we carry with us the burden of the Lord for this lost world. Of course there is a seriousness about us, a sobriety born of a deep concern for the glory of God and the salvation of sinners. But Christians are also given the gift of joy. We can and should enjoy the blessings of this life more deeply and truly than our unbelieving friends.

Nevertheless, there is a faraway look in the eyes of every lover of Jesus. There is a longing for another country. There is a deep sense that there must be *more* than the very best this world can offer. The follower of Jesus has had but a first taste of eternity. He has had a foretaste of a heavenly banquet. There is an unrest in his soul that nothing in this world can satisfy. He understands Solomon's insight into the root of our discontent:

> He has also set eternity in their heart.
> (Ecclesiastes 3:11, NASB)

My children, if you think that you can find ultimate happiness and fulfillment in this life, then you are setting yourself up for a grand and bitter disappointment. I can remember (and your mother will echo this in her own experience), coming to a place where, even having the marriage, family, career, and creature comforts I wanted (everything this world strives for), I still had a longing in my heart. Clearly, the best things this life had to give me, even the blessings of this life that God had graciously lavished upon me, were incapable of quenching the deep thirst of my soul.

The Bible teaches that Jesus is better than the best of this life. Knowing the Giver is better than any of the gifts. I would suggest that understanding this frees us up to:

1) Really love the things of this life (family, friends, possessions) with great joy and freedom, because we are no longer expecting of them what they were never designed and intended to deliver: ultimate happiness.

2) Live lives of abandonment for Jesus, not being concerned for how long we live, how comfortably we live, or whether we are valued, understood, esteemed, credited, famous enough, loved enough, or treated well enough.

Look at it this way. If Jesus' love is better than life, then the fact that He has proven His love for us on the cross (Romans 5:8) needs to be the foundation and structure of our lives. Any other love that comes our way, say through friends and family, is a bonus...but it will always be flawed. Don't expect too much from it. The sooner you get this the sooner you will be happy.

We need to hold our hearts to the flame of Christ's love for us. We need to declare our agreement with the Word of God, that "His love is better than life." This is radical, but it is also normal. This is where we need to live. Repentance, discipleship, and sacrifice become possible, and our lives gain a godly perspective.

My heroes and heroines—Hudson Taylor, William Borden, Amy Carmichael, Tessa Gillespie, Jonathan Edwards, Jackie Pullinger, Adoniram Judson, Telemachus, John Patton, Graham Staines (my list could go on and on)—all were (or are) followers of Jesus who got (or get) this. Understanding that their souls were made for the Lord, that this life was incapable of satisfying their deepest longings, they became free followers of Him whose love is better than life. Each one could have written the following words:

> I only know that in every city the Holy Spirit warns me that prison and hardships are facing me. However, I consider my life worth nothing to me; my only aim is to finish the race and complete the task the Lord Jesus has given me—the task of testifying to the good news of God's grace. (Acts 20:23-24)

What is it about this love that makes it better than life? I would suggest three things:

1) **Its source.** This love comes from Jesus Christ Himself. Its spring is deep in the eternal heart of the Triune God, sourced in who God is. No human love, be it ever so wonderful, can ever be as deep as this love.

2) **Its surety.** This love, being sourced in the very nature of God—Father, Son, Holy Spirit—is therefore not subject to change. It will not ever diminish, is not subject to moods, and will never run low. It will never be in shortage.

3) **Its substance.** This is divine love: "Love divine all loves excelling." It drew salvation's plan. It is so solid that it will be the theme song of eternity. You can stand upon it.

Some years ago, a little gem of a book came my way, *The Life of God in the Soul of Man.* Its author, Henry Scougal, died in 1657, at the ripe old age of 27. This godly young man, spiritually mature beyond his years, left to us this slim volume that has comforted, instructed, and challenged millions. The thesis of the book is simple, yet profound: The health and goodness of your soul will be determined by the excellency of that which it loves most. To love vain and sordid things is to sicken your soul unto death. To love that which is most excellent of all is to bring life and health to your inner being. To know and experience the Lord Jesus and His love is to choose to receive from Him the very best. Degrading yourself with lesser loves brings tragic ruin. Scougal writes: "the most solid and substantial delights that human nature is capable of, are those which arise from the endearments of a well-placed and successful affection...What is a little skin-deep beauty, or some small degrees of goodness, to match or satisfy a passion which was made for God; designed to embrace an infinite God?"[24]

Nurturing your soul until it becomes a fully alive *Godward* soul requires deliberate decision...every day. It means that you determine to fetch all the grace that you can to know Christ and His Love, and that you continually guard yourself against misplacing your affections and putting anything where only Christ belongs.

Learn to meditate upon the love of God displayed in Jesus Christ. Open your Bible, get on your knees, beg Heaven's help, and refuse to be refused. Get to the place where you can heartily and joyfully say that God's love is better than life itself. Weigh up the very best that this life can offer, consider it all yours for the next one hundred years, and then balance it against the love of God in Jesus for you. Dwell upon the wonders of God's love until the scale tips in His favour. Consider the amazing fact that Jesus Himself wants the very love that His Father has for Him to be in you (John 17:26). Press through until you can *feel* something of this love. Make Christ and His love for you your highest treasure and your deepest love.

I join with the Apostle Paul in praying for you that "out of His glorious riches," Christ will give you increased grace to:

> ...grasp how wide and long and high and deep is the love of Christ, and to know this love that surpasses knowledge—that you may be filled to the measure of all the fullness of God. (Ephesians 3:18, 19)

Here is a hymn, all but forgotten. Though rarely sung, it is one of my favourites because there is a depth to it. I guess it is understandable that a culture devoted to the shallow should disregard it:

****

O the Deep, Deep Love of Jesus

O the deep, deep love of Jesus, vast, unmeasured, boundless, free!
Rolling as a mighty ocean in its fullness over me!
Underneath me, all around me, is the current of Thy love
Leading onward, leading homeward to Thy glorious rest above!

O the deep, deep love of Jesus, spread His praise from shore to shore!
How He loveth, ever loveth, changeth never, nevermore!
How He watches o'er His loved ones, died to call them all His own;
How for them He intercedeth, watcheth o'er them from the throne!

O the deep, deep love of Jesus, love of every love the best!
'Tis an ocean full of blessing, 'tis a haven giving rest!
O the deep, deep love of Jesus, 'tis a heaven of heavens to me;
And it lifts me up to glory, for it lifts me up to Thee!
(Samuel T. Francis, 1834-1925)

Letter 12

Behold Him Who Is Your Strength

My grace is sufficient for you, for my power is made perfect in weakness.
2 Corinthians 12:9

Dear Ones,

You can be strong in yourself, or strong in Jesus—one or the other. You cannot be both, and you need to make a choice. If you will, you can ask the Lord to help you make this choice. If you don't ask, He will probably do it anyway. Let me tell you some of my story.

I was always very strong in myself. I could not understand people who spoke of weakness and struggle. My unspoken attitude was, "man up," or "get over it." I thought that I was a major blessing to the work of Christ, and that I had done Jesus a real favour by deciding to follow Him. His Kingdom was sure to prosper with me as one of His premier disciples!

How patient is the Lord (and His Church)! What conceited foolishness He, and my many Christian brothers and sisters, had to put up with! How many times must the Lord Jesus have rolled His eyes over me! Oh yes, I was "saved"...but a textbook immature, "baby" Christian ("obnoxious" would be a good description). If there had been a "Fellowship of Christian Jerks," I think I might have made president!

God began to reduce me. He does this to those whom He dearly loves, to those for whom He has good dreams and hopes, plans, and purposes. Yes, He is a loving God, but His love is sometimes a tough, sanctifying love. Jesus often breaks things before He uses them: bread and fish, vials of perfume, people.

There is a very revealing verse tucked away in the book of Joshua. It is one of those verses you tend to just read over. But it actually gives depth and insight into how the Lord works in those whom He has chosen:

> I assigned the hill country of Seir to Esau, but Jacob and his family
> went down to Egypt. (Joshua 24:4b)

Jacob (vice-president of the FCJ), was the chosen heir to the covenant blessings of God. Esau was not. God quickly gives Esau the vast and pleasant hill country of Seir, but takes His covenant son, Jacob, to the hardship of Egypt where he will be enslaved, reduced, and crushed. In Egypt, Jacob's family and descendants would be reshaped into a people who belong to God Himself...usable in His redemptive purposes.

Are you sure you want to follow Jesus? You can have the pleasant hill country of Seir right now. Should you follow Jesus, He will probably take you to Egypt. He will reduce you and weaken you. You asked for a loving God, and you have one in Jesus. But this is *real* love—not just sentiment. It is strong, redemptive, and it reshapes us. God loves us enough to accept us just as we are, but too much to leave us that way.

The way it works is this: We are selfish, ruined creatures. He sets His redeeming love upon us for no reason other than that His sovereign wisdom, goodness, and mercy deign it...and He means business. If He has to take us apart to make us right, He will. If you come to Him as a broken mess, He will put you back together. But if you, like me, come to Him as a self-assured good guy who is certain that he is doing God a great favour just by "deciding to follow Jesus," God will most likely have to break you, diminish you, and weaken you. He does not do this with Esau because He has no redemptive purpose with Esau. This is precisely why so many unbelievers seem to have it so good. They do have it good, in the short term. They have Seir while you have Egypt; but Seir is all they ever get. You will get a Land of Promise. Go have a diligent reading of Psalm 73.

Back to my story. I was once fearless. Cocky, self-confident, ready to change the world. Now, this works fine in certain theatres of life, but it gets in the way of the work of the Holy Spirit. The Christian life is a *super*natural life, and when one is too amazed at his natural self, God has to intervene. Jacob had to have his hip dislocated, and he limped from then on. Esau did not limp. God touched me at the very point of my strength: My confidence. At a moment in time in 1978 (I could take you to the exact place), He "dislocated" my self confidence. It happened when I was all alone, and least expecting it. He began to reduce me. In fact, over the next few years, He ground me to powder. It was unbelievably painful. I lost every bit of my "self" confidence. I was pressed to Jesus' side...tremblingly close. For all the pain, my walk with Jesus Christ grew more precious than ever before.

That experience left me with a limp, but I bless the Lord for this. You will know that I was further weakened with a "nervous breakthrough" (sometimes called a "nervous breakdown"). In all of this, I have discovered the strength of Jesus. If I were still strong, striding about in my Jacob strength, I would not know His power in the same way. I used to bound "up" into the pulpit...in my own strength. Now I step "down" into the pulpit, from the presence of the Lord, weak, but strengthened. Everything is harder, and everything is so much more precious.

C.S. Lewis' autobiographical poem, "As the Ruin Falls," tells us of God dismantling him through the trials of life and love. It is unspeakably insightful as it resolves itself in these words:

> For this I bless you as the ruin falls. The pains
> You give me are more precious than all other gains.[25]

Likewise, the Apostle Paul tells us he had a spiritual experience too wonderful for words:

> I know a man in Christ who fourteen years ago was caught up to the third heaven. Whether it was in the body or out of the body I do not know—God knows. And I know that this man—whether in the body or apart from the body I do not know, but God knows—was caught up to paradise and heard inexpressible things, things that no one is permitted to tell. (2 Corinthians 12:2-4)

Because Jesus loved Paul, and was concerned that this experience might lead to spiritual pride, He used Satan to afflict him, to humble him, for his own good and the good of the Gospel. God knows that a self-assured, egotistical man is a danger to himself and to His Kingdom. Paul tells us that three times, he asked the Lord to take this particular unnamed affliction away from him, but God would not! The Lord's answer is deep, moving, and glorious:

> Three times I pleaded with the Lord to take it away from me. But he said to me, "My grace is sufficient for you, for my power is made perfect in weakness." (2 Corinthians 12:8, 9)

Are you seeing here that the Apostle Paul was actually in a *better place* when weak in himself? For then, he was strong in Jesus Christ:

> Therefore I will boast all the more gladly about my weaknesses, so that Christ's power may rest on me. That is why, for Christ's sake, I delight in weaknesses, in insults, in hardships, in persecutions, in difficulties. For when I am weak, then I am strong. (2 Corinthians 12:9b-10)

You are never in a better place than when you are on your knees before the Lord, desperately aware of your weaknesses and asking in desperate faith for His strength to be manifested in you. D.L. Moody said, "True faith is man's weakness leaning on God's strength." A key to fullness and spiritual power is confessing emptiness and spiritual weakness. Feast on the following:

> I love you, O Lord, *my strength*. (Psalm 18:1)
>
> The Lord is *my strength*. (Psalm 28:7)
>
> The Lord *gives strength* to His people. (Psalm 29:11)
>
> Blessed are those whose *strength is in you*. (Psalm 84:5)
>
> I can do everything through Him who gives *me strength*. (Philippians 4:13)
>
> Whose weakness was *turned to strength*. (Hebrews 11:34)
>
> If anyone serves...do it with the *strength God provides*. (1 Peter 4:11)

It is vital that we surrender to the reducing work of the Lord in our lives. We must submit to His greater purposes when the Lord decides that we are too self-reliant. If we kick and squirm, demanding and darting, we may become wearied but not weakened. We may end up bitter but not better. Paul did not say: "Three times I asked Jesus to remove this thorn, and He did not! I am sick of this and Him! No more following Jesus for me!" No, he submitted and surrendered. The end result was a weaker, but better man—a man whose strength was now in the ever able God, and not in the man.

Dear children of mine, I ask you to dare to trust the Lord Jesus enough to ask Him to break you. This Christian life is a life in the Spirit. It is truly not about our amazing natural abilities, but about Him working through weak and available servants. "We have this treasure in jars of clay to show that this all-surpassing power is from God and not from us" (2 Corinthians 4:7). It is about Jesus being ministered, through us. It is about a work of the Spirit and not of the flesh.

Jesus Christ is not short on strength! Behold Him who is your strength. Rebuke your own powers, get on your knees, and ask the Lord to be strong through you. Take your weaknesses and offer them up to the Lord. Ask the Lord and then trust Him to work a work in you that is impossible without Him. Don't ask for an easy life, but rather for a life that displays His grace and strength at work in you. Seek a supernatural life, a life lived in the power of God.

Don't pray for a life that matches your strength. Pray for strength to match the upward call of God. Believe for a miracle life. Dream dreams that demand God comes through or you face-plant. Seek a life on the edge, beyond what you can do. Anyone can become a millionaire, a movie star, a sports hero. These are all natural things. Only broken people can be used by the Eternal God for supernatural works. Reflecting back upon a life profoundly used by Jesus, Hudson Taylor said:

> I sometimes think that God was looking for someone small enough and weak enough, so that when used, Jesus would be sure to get all of the glory, and that He found me.[26]

Believe for the impossible, submit yourself to God's greatest purposes for your life, and then see what God can do in and through you. Trust that life's trials and tribulations are actually the Father's hand shaping your life, weakening your reliance on yourself and strengthening you in Him. Desire spiritual strength over your own and see what God will do though a submitted and surrendered clay pot.

Many years ago, I read Elisabeth Elliot's biography of Amy Carmichael, *A Chance to Die: The Life and Legacy of Amy Carmichael*. Deep within those pages I read for the first time these arresting words:

> From pray'r that asks that I may be
> Sheltered from winds that beat on Thee,
> From fearing when I should aspire,
> From falt'ring when I should climb high'r,
> From silken self, O Captain, free
> Thy soldier who would follow Thee.
>
> From subtle love of softening things,
> From easy choices, weakenings,

(Not thus are spirits fortified,
Not this way went the Crucified),
From all that dims Thy Calvary,
O Lamb of God, deliver me.

Give me the love that leads the way,
The faith that nothing can dismay,
The hope no disappointments tire,
The passion that will burn like fire,
Let me not sink to be a clod:
Make me Thy fuel, O flame of God.
(Amy Carmichael, 1867-1951)[27]

These words (in fact, that whole volume), were essential to my early spiritual formation, helping me to see that God's purposes were to reshape me, like a physician breaking a wrongly set bone, that he might skilfully set it aright, for my good and His glory.

God delights to reduce His children, not because He is cruel, but because He is genuinely loving. Sin has so distorted us, so puffed us up, that we—like a bone broken and wrongly set—must be *re*-broken so that the Great Physician might set us straight. Old-timers understood this better than we do because they were better theologians. They understood that we are deeply depraved and must undergo major surgery at the soul level if we are to get to the place where we despair of ourselves and our strength and humbly look to the Lord moment by moment as our strength and help.

Would you dare pray, "Lord Jesus, lover of my soul, break me, reduce me, and bring me to a place where you and you alone are my all sufficient strength and help?"

I leave you once again with the great words of Isaac Watts. Oh, to know the Lord as did these men and women of old. Oh, to swim in great rivers of truth as did those great minds:

****

O God Our Help

Our God, our help in ages past,
Our hope for years to come,
Our shelter from the stormy blast,
And our eternal home.

Under the shadow of Thy throne
Thy saints have dwelt secure;
Sufficient is Thine arm alone,
And our defense is sure.

Before the hills in order stood,
Or earth received her frame,
From everlasting Thou art God,
To endless years the same.

Thy Word commands our flesh to dust,
"Return, ye sons of men:"
All nations rose from earth at first,
And turn to earth again.

A thousand ages in Thy sight
Are like an evening gone;
Short as the watch that ends the night
Before the rising sun.

The busy tribes of flesh and blood,
With all their lives and cares,
Are carried downwards by the flood,
And lost in following years.

Time, like an ever flowing stream
Bears all its sons away.
They fly forgotten as a dream
Dies at the opening day.

Like flowery fields the nations stand
Pleased with the morning light;
The flowers beneath the mower's hand
Lie withering ere 'tis night.

Our God, our help in ages past,
Our hope for years to come,
Be Thou our guard while troubles last,
And our eternal home.
(Isaac Watts, 1674-1748)

Letter 13

Behold the One Who Divides

Thus the people were divided because of Jesus. John 7:43

Dear Ones,

People get sentimental over Jesus. It is tempting to reshape Him into someone palatable, tame, and blunt. People do not mind a tepid Jesus who makes His tepid followers a bit more comfortable. What J.I. Packer observed as "hot tub religion" is alive and well. Countless professed believers are happily bubbling away their precious years. Such disciples make no enemies with a world that crucified their professed Saviour. Likewise, no one really minds if you have a bit of private faith, the more vague the better. Neither passion nor precision is welcome these days, where Jesus is concerned. It is considered rude and narrow to be "sure," especially about Jesus. C.S. Lewis' quote "got me" right at the start of my Christian journey, nearly forty years ago:

> Christianity, if false, is of no importance, and if true, of infinite importance, the only thing it cannot be is moderately important.[28]

The Jesus of the Bible is not some fuzzy religious figure from the dim past. The Bible does not belong on the shelf with Mother Goose, nor on the religion and philosophy shelf, but on the history shelf. The witnesses in the Bible invite our investigation; they welcome our scrutiny. Fearlessly, they challenge us to *believe* in Jesus, leaving all lesser "gods" behind. So Dr. Luke, the Bible's ace historian, begins his history of Jesus this way:

Many have undertaken to draw up an account of the things that have
been fulfilled among us, just as they were handed down to us by those
who from the first were eyewitnesses and servants of the word. With
this in mind, since I myself have carefully investigated everything
from the beginning, I too decided to write an orderly account for you,
most excellent Theophilus, so that you may know the certainty of the
things you have been taught.
(Luke 1:1-4)

Likewise, Peter, the meat and potatoes fisherman, writes:

We did not follow cleverly devised stories when we told you about
the coming of our Lord Jesus Christ in power, but we were eyewitnesses of his majesty. (2 Peter 1:16)

John, the rough and ready "Son of Thunder," tells us:

That which was from the beginning, which we have heard, which
we have seen with our eyes, which we have looked at and our hands
have touched—this we proclaim concerning the Word of life. The life
appeared; we have seen it and testify to it, and we proclaim to you
the eternal life, which was with the Father and has appeared to us. We
proclaim to you what we have seen and heard, so that you also may
have fellowship with us. And our fellowship is with the Father and
with his Son, Jesus Christ.
(1 John 1:1-3)

These men—soon to be martyrs—were convinced that Jesus was
the Son of God, the Truth, the only way to Heaven and they presented
Him to their world with do-or-die passion, no matter what the personal cost. They won no popularity contests. They did not care to.
Their message stirred things up wherever they went.

These men have turned our world upside down!

Do not speak any more in this name!

Read the Book of Acts and see what Jesus does! Revivals and riots go together in the world of the New Testament. Why? What is it about Jesus and His message that divides? Don't we want everyone to be happy and everyone to have a good time? Shouldn't "true religion" bring everyone together? This is what the world tells us! Why doesn't Jesus?

The thing about Jesus that grates is the *exclusivity* of His claims. His "I AM" declarations in John's Gospel alone are enough to put Him at odds with both a Roman world that paid its homage to Caesar and a modern world that insists that truth is relative, unknowable, and equally distributed between all religions and ideologies.

But when Jesus says:

> "I am the:
> Way
> Truth
> Life
> Light of the world
> Door
> Bread of life
> Resurrection
> Good Shepherd,"

He is not only saying something about Himself, He is also saying something about everyone else. He is saying that *no one else* is the Way, Truth, Life, etc. He thus identifies all who make alternative truth claims as pretenders, deceivers, false teachers, blind guides, and confused confusers. He is boldly asserting that what people think about *Him* is the crucial issue of life:

> Whoever believes in the Son has eternal life, but whoever rejects the Son will not see life, for God's wrath remains on them. (John 3:36)

These words, straight from the lips of Jesus, and many other words like them, are astounding, and we need to recover their shock value. They tell us that God has acted decisively in Jesus to save sinners, and by implication, not in Buddha, Krishna, Mohammed, or any other. They tell us that He is the dividing line of humanity, that all are hopeless, torbid, miserable offenders, and that all who "believe in the Son" are relieved of their sins and delivered from God's wrath.

Likewise, the witness of the otherwise blundering apostles was clear and uncompromised:

> Salvation is found in no one else, for there is no other name under heaven given to mankind by which we must be saved. (Acts 4:12)

> We cannot help speaking about what we have seen and heard. (Acts 4:20)

> I am not ashamed of the gospel, because it is the power of God that brings salvation to everyone who believes: first to the Jew, then to the Gentile. (Romans 1:16)

> Whoever has the Son has life; whoever does not have the Son of God does not have life. (1 John 5:12)

My dear ones, I have said it before, but I must say again that the greatest battle the Christian Church will face in this century will be over the issue of Jesus Christ Himself. (We dare not battle over a lesser issue). That is, who He is, and what He does. Is He the unique Son of the Living God, and does He alone secure salvation for sinners? As it was in the first century, so shall it be in the twenty-first. Christians will come under great pressure to say that Jesus is one among many. No one will mind you believing that Jesus is "a way." This will even be fashionable. But to say that Jesus Christ alone is the hope of sinners will increasingly get you into hot water. But this is precisely what we must do. Anything less is unfaithfulness to our God and our generation.

It is not about *us* being "right," but about *Christ* being the truth. Our message is not, "we are the right ones," but, "Christ is Saviour and Lord, the sinner's only hope. Repent of all other hopes and trust in Him." Never confuse confidence and arrogance. Arrogance is a detestable accessory to a Christian's wardrobe. Arrogance says, "I am right, and if you were like me, the world would be a better place." Arrogance draws attention to itself. Confidence is altogether different. It adorns the Christian with humble assurance, draws attention not to itself but to Christ and His Gospel. Confidence says, "Christ is a faithful Saviour and the Lord of all. Repent and believe in Him and you shall have life." Confidence shines the spotlight upon Christ, arrogance, upon self. We dare not be arrogant. We must be confident.

Nevertheless, confidence in Christ, be it ever so self-effacing and humble, will get you in trouble in today's world. Our culture does not even believe in the category "Truth," let alone that Christ occupies it.[29] We applaud confusion and see fogginess as a virtue. Remember what Ravi Zacharias observed, that in today's climate you can believe anything you want, so long as you don't believe it is *true*. Our challenge is and will be to humbly, lovingly, but boldly present Christ to our generation as the only hope for the ruined human race, and not flinch when they begin to throw stones.

Jesus said, "Do you think I came to bring peace on earth? No, I tell you, but division. From now on there will be five in one family divided against each other, three against two and two against three" (Luke 12:51, 52).

These are not "nice" words, because Jesus is not "nice." Like Aslan, He is not safe, but He is good. All the acceptable "Jesuses"— Jesus the guru, Jesus the teacher, Jesus the prophet, Jesus the martyr, Jesus the social activist—are all nice Jesuses. But they are incomplete. They are inoffensive. They are too blunt to divide. None of them can cut and separate. The Bible's Jesus:

> *Spoke with divine authority
> (Matthew 24:35; 28:18)

*Claimed the authority to forgive sins

(Mark 2:10)

*Made Himself to be the conscious focus of saving faith

(Luke 14:26)

*Took titles reserved only for God

(John 8:12; 10:1)

*Received honour and worship due only to God

(John 5:23; 17:1, 5)

*Claimed for Himself a unique relationship with the Father

(John 8:49; 10:30)

*Claimed to be the judge of all mankind

(John 5:27; Matthew 25:31)

*Claimed that our eternal destinies were dependent upon Him

(Mark 8:35-37)

*Claimed for Himself eternal existence

(John 8:58)

May the Lord give us grace to love Jesus, others, and the Gospel more than we love our lives. I am reading the new Bonhoeffer biography as I write these words.[30] One thing became increasingly clear to this young follower of Jesus as the Hitler terror gained traction: The time came when being orthodox was not enough. There came a time when one had to move from mere *confession* of Christ, to defiant *resistance* to the spirit of the age. One had to become a *conspirator against evil* to be a faithful follower of Jesus. So it is today. The spirit of the age is telling us to go private with our testimony in the name of tolerance, to no longer hold to the uniqueness of Jesus, to sacrifice the Gospel on the altar of political correctness. It is time to be not just those who confess in privacy and safety, but in defiance of what is acceptable, to be those who proclaim Christ in the streets, universities, media, and danger spots of this world. Anything less is faithless disobedience.

Our generation thinks it is finished with Jesus, when in fact it has yet to deal with Him. Our glorious and costly calling is to proclaim Him to our generation faithfully, humbly, boldly, incessantly, confidently, joyfully, and earnestly *no matter the cost,* until we behold Him face to face.

Here is a great Wesley hymn which deserves another chance. Compared to most of us, the Wesleys and company were men (and women) of steel. It was not unusual for them to be dragged through the gutter and beaten by an angry mob, only to stand again and preach the wonders of Christ to that same mob. Make this hymn a prayer:

****

Give Me the Faith Which Can Remove

Give me the faith which can remove
And sink the mountain to a plain;
Give me the childlike praying love,
Which longs to build Thy house again;
Thy love, let it my heart overpower,
And all my simple soul devour.

I want an even strong desire,
I want a calmly fervent zeal,
To save poor souls out of the fire,
To snatch them from the verge of hell,
And turn them to a pardoning God,
And quench the brands in Jesus' blood.

I would the precious time redeem,
And longer live for this alone,
To spend and to be spent for them
Who have not yet my Savior known;
Fully on these my mission prove,
And only breathe, to breathe Thy love.

My talents, gifts, and graces, Lord,
Into Thy blessed hands receive;
And let me live to preach Thy Word,
And let me to Thy glory live;
My every sacred moment spend
In publishing the sinner's Friend.

Enlarge, inflame, and fill my heart
With boundless charity divine,
So shall I all strength exert,
And love them with a zeal like Thine,
And lead them to Thy open side,
The sheep for whom the Shepherd died.
(Charles Wesley, 1707-1788)

Letter 14

Behold Him Who Is True Humanity

Is not this the carpenter's son? Is not His mother called Mary,
and His brothers, James and Joseph and Simon and Judas?
Matthew 13:55 (NASB)

Dear Ones,

I remember many years ago being struck by Karl Barth's observation that true humanity, that is, what it really means to be human, cannot be discovered by looking to anyone except Jesus Christ. He is *the* perfect and true human. The secular slogan is, "The proper study of mankind is man." I say, "No, the proper study of mankind is Jesus." If you want to discover what it means to be a person, study Jesus. Fully God, "very God of very God," but fully man. Emmanuel, God with us, incarnate, but at the same time, a man. A man in every way.

We are looking in the wrong direction when we look to *each other* to try and understand what it means to be human. We are *fallen*, and therefore *abnormal*. Sin corrupts, mars, and defaces. Never confuse the common with the normal. It is *common* to see sinful, fallen humanity. It is all around us and within us. But *normal* humanity is not sinful. Humans were made for fellowship with God. And there is one, only one *normal* human that has ever lived: Jesus Christ. It is as we behold Him that we understand what it means to be human. We must draw our example from Him.

Rather than write a systematic essay about the humanity of Jesus, I want to focus on one or two episodes from His life. Marvel with me, and adore the humanness of Jesus.

> Then he (Jesus) went down to Nazareth with them and was obedient
> to them. But His mother treasured all these things in her heart. And
> Jesus grew in wisdom and stature, and in favor with God and man.
> (Luke 2:51, 52)

Now, theologians have long contemplated just what it actually meant for Jesus to "empty Himself" of His "divine prerogatives" (that is, leave Heaven and come as a human to Earth). The bottom line is that we really cannot comprehend such a condescension. The best we can do is marvel and worship. But to not understand a truth fully is not to say we cannot understand it partly, and to grasp a magnificent truth in part can be life transforming.

Dr. Luke, the writer of the Gospel that bears his name, offers a brief but profound description of Jesus during His teenage years. It is deep in insight and significance in regards to the miracle of the Incarnation. It gives us the only information we have of the Lord Jesus during His teenage and young adult years.

It is clear from Luke that by the time Jesus was twelve years old, He knew something of His unique relationship to His Heavenly Father, and of His life being given over to His Father's will. We find the boy (young man) Jesus conversing with the elders in the temple for three days while Joseph and Mary were looking for Him. Remember His profound statement to His parents upon their discovery of Him in the temple:

> Didn't you know I had to be in my Father's House?
> (Luke 2:49)

So, here we have the incarnate Son of God, emerging into human adulthood. Clearly something of His uniqueness was dawning upon His conscience. This is precisely the point at which, if this were a Hindu, Buddhist, or New Age story, the boy Jesus would have been exalted to a venerable position as a boy wonder, taken out of normal life altogether, put on a pillow, and deified.

This is precisely what *did not* happen to the adolescent Jesus.

Look at Dr. Luke's story (no doubt received directly from Mary herself):

> Then he went down to Nazareth with them and was obedient to them. But his mother treasured all these things in her heart. (Luke 2:51)

Marvel with me at how *human* this account is! It helps us to see just how *earthy* the incarnate Christ was. Jesus did not enter a shrine or monastery. They did not make posters of Him:

"Come see the amazing God-Boy!"

He went *home* and *obeyed* his parents, notwithstanding that in the eternal scheme of things, *they* owed *Him* their very existence (John 1:3)! *He* was subject to *them* and this honored His Heavenly Father. This Jesus is no "ghost." This is a real, meaty Incarnation.

Luke then tells us of the fourfold maturing of the young teen to manhood. Use his words to allow your sanctified imagination to ponder and enjoy (and wonder at) the miracle of God in human flesh:

And He grew in wisdom. Jesus grew *intellectually.* The young man submitted Himself to the Scriptures which are able to make one wise (2 Timothy 3:15), and to His elders, for he who walks with the wise becomes wise (Proverbs 13:20). The lad did His homework. He took exams. He studied. He who knew the secrets of the universe had to learn His sums! Now, I cannot figure this out...I just marvel at it.

And in stature. He grew *physically.* He did His press-ups. His biceps grew and His shoulders broadened. His voice deepened, and He went through puberty. Jesus was not a wimp. He was a construction worker. He could lift, he grunted, and hauled stuff around. His hands grew strong and calloused. Consider this: Eternal God, the Son whose hands flung stars into space, had a time when, as a human boy, He could not quite lift a hundred weight of sand. Then, a few thousand press-ups and a month or two of Mom's good meals later, he had no problem carrying a bag on each shoulder!

And in favor with God. He grew *spiritually*. Here we have the Eternal Son of God, very God of very God, somehow in the mystery of the Incarnation, learning to pray and read His Torah and have a meaningful quiet time. He had to be disciplined. He had to desire to know the Lord in depth. He memorized scriptures—scriptures of which He was the author and Incarnation ("the Word became Flesh and dwelt among us," John 1:14), and which "testify of" Him (John 5:39). Wonder of wonders!

And in favor with men. He grew *socially*. He was no wallflower. He learned to mix and mingle. People liked having Him around. He never sinned to fit in, but He could fit in with sinners. He learned good manners and how to conduct Himself politely in company. I can imagine the Lord Jesus being able to discuss, debate, laugh, and engage with His peers. I can see Him empathizing with them in their trials and rejoicing with them in their triumphs. Indeed, the proverb, "A wise son brings joy to his father," (Proverbs 10:1) was true of the young Jesus.

So we discover from Dr. Luke's brief biography of the teenage Jesus that the Incarnation was, in fact, deep and rich. The "emptying" of the Eternal Son of God was thorough. Perhaps Charles Wesley, the hymn writer, has gone where most theologians dared not go, but got closer to the truth than they:

Emptied Himself of all but love...

God in Christ has completely come among us. This was not a phantom appearance, but a true and real Incarnation. And this same Jesus became for us "a merciful and faithful High Priest in service to God" (Hebrews 2:17), for He who "emptied Himself of all but love":

Bled for Adam's helpless race.

I am an adorer of the mystery. It is all beyond me, but I receive it and wonder at it: God becoming man—earthy, real, sweaty, hungry, thirsty...and *sinless*.

> Our God contracted to a span,
> Incomprehensibly made man.

"Super-spirituality" cannot cope with the earthiness that is true Christianity. But the Bible makes holy the humdrum, through the Incarnation of God, in Christ. Eating, sleeping, laughing, working, crying, parties, weddings, funerals and more are all now valuable and sacred, because *God did all these things*. Take a look at one other episode in the earthly ministry of Jesus. We move from the adolescent to the risen and glorified Christ—risen not as a ghost but as the glorified man. Here we find Him in John's Gospel, the scene is the shoreline of Galilee:

> When they landed, they saw a fire of burning coals there with fish on it, and some bread. Jesus said to them, "Bring some of the fish you have just caught." (John 21:9, 10)

The disciples landed their boats to find Jesus, the risen Lord, not hovering a foot or two above the sand, but with a fire kindled and breakfast on the go. HE MADE THEM BREAKFAST! How *normal*. How *unspiritual*. How *wonderful*. The risen Lord cares about His disciples' stomachs. I love the earthiness of this scene. Again, the ordinary is hallowed by Jesus. He is declaring this world to be of grand importance, this life as valuable to God, and therefore to be valued by us.

Jesus, the human, warns us not to try to be more spiritual than God has wired us to be. We see in Him no separation between the sacred and secular. It is *all* sacred to Jesus. Everything is flowing from a heart satisfied in His Heavenly Father. Christian spirituality is profoundly normal because Jesus embodies life in all its sweat, grit, joy, and sorrow.

Here is a beautiful hymn that I remember fondly from my childhood in Brazil. I can so vividly recall standing close to my mother in
church as a little boy, singing these earthy, holy words:

****

This Is My Father's World

This is my Father's world
And to my listening ears
All nature sings and round me rings
The music of the spheres

This is my Father's world
I rest me in the thought
Of rocks, of trees, of skies and seas
His hand the wonders wrought

This is my Father's world
Oh, and let me never forget
That though the wrong seems often so strong
God is the ruler yet

This is my Father's world,
the birds their carols raise,
the morning light, the lily white,
declare their maker's praise.

This is my Father's world:
He shines in all that's fair;
in the rustling grass I hear him pass;
He speaks to me everywhere.

This is my Father's world
Oh, the battle is not done
Jesus who died will be satisfied
And the earth, heaven will be one
(Maltbie Babcock, 1858-1901)

Letter 15

Behold Him Who Bids You to Abide

He who abides in Me and I in him, he bears much fruit, for apart from Me you can do nothing. John 15:5 (NASB)

My Dear Children,

Oh, the wonders of a God who bids us to stick close to His side! Ours is not a God who grows weary of His children, sending them away in an exasperated huff. "Abide with me" is the welcome invitation of Jesus to each of you. Here is an invitation to attachment, a willingness on the part of God to have you tag along in His adventure.

"Abide" is a deep, rich, beautiful word. It means, "to dwell with," "to remain or continue." It is an intimate and living word. It is relational. It is a patient word that is not in a hurry. Eugene Peterson translates this verse as:

> When you're joined with me and I with you, the relation intimate and organic, the harvest is sure to be abundant.[31]

Jesus knows that the key to our lives is our relationship with Him: "Apart from me you can do nothing" (John 15:5). All fruitfulness, all ministry, all fullness is directly dependent upon our relationship with Christ. This Christian life is a divine life. It is about Jesus living His life in us as we abide in Him. It is not about how busy we are but how quiet we are, for "abide" is a slow word. It does not do well in the fast lane. Jesus *wants* a relationship with you, though He does not *need* it. Though He is complete in His relationship with His Father and the Spirit, He chooses to seek relationship with us. We, however, *need* to abide in Him for our very survival.

There is an organic necessity that the branch has towards the vine. There is a sense of desperation here. It is as if the branch *knows* that it derives its whole life from the vine. It has absolutely no life in itself. "Apart from me you can do nothing." Jesus does not mean we cannot become millionaires, movie stars, or achieve any one of a number of other mundane triumphs. He is speaking here of weightier things, things of eternal consequence, things pertaining to the Kingdom of God. Jesus is telling us that unless we remain in Him, we will not and cannot have any significant fruit produced in our lives.

Way back in 1982, when your mother and I were first married and living in Dallas, we got wind that the aged saint, Leonard Ravenhill, was living with his dear wife about 100 miles east of us in Lindale. After repeated attempts to get an hour of his time, he finally agreed to meet us in his home. "Come with your questions," he said, "and let's not waste time looking at my books."

He and his wife welcomed us warmly, and this dear man, whose book *Why Revival Tarries,* had made such an impact upon me, spoke words of wisdom into our young lives. One thing stuck in my mind above all others. Ravenhill said: "You take care of the depth of your life with Jesus and let Him build the ministry. Your first and greatest concern has to be your relationship with Christ." I have never forgotten that advice. My concern is to abide with Christ, not to build a ministry. My priority is to look to Him daily for grace, guidance, wisdom, and strength. My preeminent focus is my walk with Christ, not my productivity.

I think you will find that keeping your heart exclusively for Christ will be your most difficult task over the course of your life. To jealously guard your heart for Jesus will prove to be the most important and most challenging thing in your life. A thousand other good things will clamour to keep you from the best. You will find that the hardest world to master is the world within. The battle in my own breast is bigger than any other I have ever faced. But the effort is always richly rewarded, and God is not slow to pour out abundant grace upon the one who is earnest to have a heart towards Him. Yet the remarkable thing is that as we abide, we produce.

Look at the progression in John 15:

*No fruit (v.2)
    *Fruit (v.2)
        *More fruit (v.2)
            *Much fruit (v.5)
                *Fruit that will last (v.16)

What a wonderful Saviour we have! He *wants* us to walk closely with Him. It is His desire that we live in intimate union with Him. He *wants* to bear His fruit through us. He welcomes us to His side, embraces us, and draws us to Himself (usually through trials).

Children, if the Devil cannot rock you to sleep, he will ride you like a horse. He will busy you with a thousand distractions, even ministries, just to keep you from abiding and remaining with Jesus. Your life with Christ is the only thing that is really yours to keep. Every earthly love and relationship will someday have to leave you. Martin Luther said it well, when he said there are two things you must do all by yourself, that no human being can do for you or with you: You must believe in Christ alone, and you must die alone. In the end, all you will have is your relationship with Jesus. And this can never be taken from you. Cherish it and value it above all else.

This beautiful Wesley hymn has ministered to millions. It is fragrant with intimacy, the intimacy born of desperation and full confidence in Christ:

****

Jesus Lover of My Soul

Jesus, lover of my soul,
let me to Thy bosom fly,
While the nearer waters roll,
while the tempest still is high.
Hide me, O my Savior, hide,

till the storm of life is past;
Safe into the haven guide;
O receive my soul at last.

Other refuge have I none,
Hangs my helpless soul on Thee;
Leave, ah! leave me not alone,
Still support and comfort me.
All my trust on Thee is stayed,
All my help from Thee I bring;
Cover my defenseless head
With the shadow of Thy wing.

Wilt Thou not regard my call?
Wilt Thou not accept my prayer?
Lo! I sink, I faint, I fall—
Lo! on Thee I cast my care.
Reach me out Thy gracious hand!
While I of Thy strength receive,
Hoping against hope I stand,
Dying, and behold, I live.

Thou, O Christ, art all I want,
More than all in Thee I find;
Raise the fallen, cheer the faint,
Heal the sick, and lead the blind.
Just and holy is Thy Name,
Source of all true righteousness;
Thou art evermore the same,
Thou art full of truth and grace.

Plenteous grace with Thee is found,
Grace to cover all my sin;
Let the healing streams abound;
Make and keep me pure within.
Thou of life the fountain art,
Freely let me take of Thee;
Spring Thou up within my heart;
Rise to all eternity.
(Charles Wesley, 1707-1788)

Letter 16

Behold Him Who Is Unsurpassed

When I saw him, I fell at his feet as though dead. Then he placed his right hand on me and said: "Do not be afraid. I am the First and the Last. I am the Living One; I was dead, and now look, I am alive for ever and ever! And I hold the keys of death and Hades. Revelation 1:17-18

My Dearest Children,

Your view of Jesus is too small. I know it is. So is mine. The deepest need in your life is to know Him better. Of this, I am absolutely certain. This is the deepest need in my life too. We get satisfied with our present experience of Jesus too quickly. I am praying for a healthy, godly *dissatisfaction* in us all!

The Apostle Paul, after years of following Jesus could still say, "I want to know Christ" (Philippians 3:10). He was not satisfied with his experience and relationship with his Saviour. Didn't he already know enough? He wrote Romans, Galatians, Ephesians, and Colossians, in a sense formulating the cardinal doctrines of Christianity. Untold thousands of books and articles have been written, unpacking the deep doctrinal truths the Apostle Paul gave to the Church. Whole movements have been birthed in response to Paul's masterful grasp and presentation of Christian truth. What more was there for this great follower of Jesus to know?

The truth is that Jesus Christ is without limit in terms of His nature and being. The Eternal God—Father, Son, and Holy Spirit—will occupy our greatest powers of thought and our greatest affections of heart for all of our days here in this life. Then, "in a nobler sweeter frame," our glorified abilities will marvel yet more at our God as our journey of discovery stretches into eternity.

> Oh, the depth of the riches of
> the wisdom and knowledge of God!
> How unsearchable his judgments,
> and his paths beyond tracing out!
>
> "Who has known the mind of the Lord?
> Or who has been his counselor?"
> "Who has ever given to God,
> that God should repay them?"
>
> For from him and through him and for him are all things.
> To him be the glory forever! Amen!
> (Romans 11:33-36)

Jesus Christ is unsurpassed in every category, except sin. We entertain views of Jesus that are far too limited. Our apprehension of Him needs to be forever expanding and deepening, growing ever more glorious. Consider with me the description of Jesus found in Paul's letter to the Colossians (a church which had grown enamoured with "super-spirituality," rules, and angels):

> The Son is the image of the invisible God, the firstborn over all
> creation. For in him all things were created: things in heaven and
> on earth, visible and invisible, whether thrones or powers or rul-
> ers or authorities; all things have been created through him and for
> him. He is before all things, and in him all things hold together. And
> he is the head of the body, the church; he is the beginning and the
> firstborn from among the dead, so that in everything he might have
> the supremacy. For God was pleased to have all his fullness dwell
> in him, and through him to reconcile to himself all things, whether
> things on earth or things in heaven, by making peace through his
> blood, shed on the cross. (Colossians 1:15-20)

If you take some time and *think* about the description of Jesus you have just read, you will discover what God the Father wants you to see about God the Son: He is supreme in every way. It is *impossible* to conceive of a being greater than He who is described in these verses...go on and try. The effort will do you good. Jesus stands absolutely alone. Line up all the great figures of history and put them on one side. Do not put Jesus of Nazareth with them. Put Him on the other side, in resplendent singularity. When you are put under pressure to equate Jesus with other "great leaders," *do not do it.* Each and every one will one day stand before Him and give an account. They are sinners, one and all, frail creatures of dust—the lot of them.

It is simply not possible to live above the level of your "gods." Little gods produce little lives. But it is as we, "with unveiled faces contemplate the Lord's glory," that we become "transformed into his image with ever-increasing glory" (2 Corinthians 3:18). We become increasingly like God or like the "gods" we worship. For example, the Hindu "gods" lie, cheat, and steal. They are just like us, only a little bigger. Hence the society which worships them cannot but do the same. For this reason, Hinduism is incapable of producing a society that values honesty and integrity in business and marriage.

Jesus alone is capable of bringing beauty to our lives at a deep level, for He is beautiful, through and through. "He will beautify the afflicted ones with salvation" (Psalm 149:4, NASB). Jesus alone can restore beauty to a ruined life. He alone can inspire to the highest goals, the grandest purposes. It is in pressing on in our experience of Christ that our lives become loosened from the tethers of the trivial, and we are increasingly liberated to a meaningful life. Just ask Jim Elliot, Mary Slessor, Dietrich Bonhoeffer, or Catherine Booth.

Are there not yet undiscovered treasures in this life with Christ— vast regions of this unsurpassed Saviour yet to explore? Have we not barely scratched the surface of the limitless mines of His redeeming love? For surely, of all the incomparable attributes of Jesus, His love outshines them all. Where else will we find a love that stretches out its hands to be nailed to a cross to die for a ruined race? Where else will we find a love which patiently waits for the sinner to "come to his senses"? Where else will we find a love which spares no pain and no cost in redeeming Adam's helpless race? Dear child, do not allow yourself to grow used to the fact that Jesus loves you. Do not lose your childlike amazement over the Gospel.

I think that because we no longer appreciate the iniquity of our sin, as a necessary consequence, we no longer truly marvel at the love of God. We are not *really* amazed that Jesus loves us, and we should be overwhelmed by the fact. But we take sin so lightly. We think it just makes us "one of the boys," or "no big deal," when in fact our sin is the scandal of the universe.

Have you ever marveled at this declaration of God: "Jacob I loved, but Esau I hated" (Romans 9:13)? What amazes you about that statement? I will tell you what amazes me. It is *not* that God hated Esau. The word used for "hate" here means, "to feel hostility or intense animosity towards." I can fully understand how our Holy God would feel hostility or intense animosity towards Esau, or me, or anyone else who is fundamentally selfish and sin-loving. I have no problem with this. What is shocking about God here is that He *loved Jacob*. Read the story (Genesis 25-35)!

Jacob was a deceptive scoundrel! His was a lifetime committed to self-centred deceit. I read the story and I see so much of myself in him. There was nothing about Jacob that compelled God to love him. Nothing winsome whatsoever. Jacob's life is a soap opera of foolish moves and unravelling results, and an unrepentant, defiant, deepening rebellion. Yet God—the God of Abraham and Isaac—sets His free, unbounded, redeeming, covenant love upon this creep of all creeps. God makes him a trophy of grace, yet another testimony to the wonders of the God we know in Jesus Christ. What grace that God would be the God of Abraham, Isaac, and *Jacob*!

Now to burst your bubble: God's love for you is not enticed by you and your delightful ways. God's love is utterly free. There is nothing irresistible emanating from you. You are naturally *not* adorable.[32] God in Christ is unspeakably wonderful to love you.

In every religion, adherents strive, sometimes painfully, to merit the approval of their (usually impersonal, aloof) god or gods. In the Bible we see that God loves us for no known reason in us. He sovereignly loves us, because love is who He is in the very depth of His being.

Oh, that we would feel the iniquity of our sin, to the end that we would feel the wonders of God's love! Oh, that we would be awestruck by the Gospel! That God would move to save a sinner through the love of Christ and the Gospel is the unsurpassed headline news of the universe, and shall be, through all eternity.

I have just recently discovered the amazing old hymn below. Don't rush your way through it, but drink in its words:

****

The Love of God

The love of God is greater far
Than tongue or pen can ever tell;
It goes beyond the highest star,
And reaches to the lowest hell;
The guilty pair, bowed down with care,
God gave His Son to win;
His erring child He reconciled,
And pardoned from his sin.

O love of God, how rich and pure!
How measureless and strong!
It shall forevermore endure
The saints' and angels' song.

When years of time shall pass away,
And earthly thrones and kingdoms fall,

When men, who here refuse to pray,
On rocks and hills and mountains call,
God's love so sure, shall still endure,
All measureless and strong;
Redeeming grace to Adam's race—
The saints' and angels' song.

Could we with ink the ocean fill,
And were the skies of parchment made,
Were every stalk on earth a quill,
And every man a scribe by trade,
To write the love of God above,
Would drain the ocean dry.
Nor could the scroll contain the whole,
Though stretched from sky to sky.

O love of God, how rich and pure!
How measureless and strong!
It shall forevermore endure
The saints' and angels' song.
(Fredrick Lehman, 1868-1953) [33]

Letter 17

Behold Him Who Is Your Comfort in
Life and in Death

Yea, though I walk through the valley of the shadow of death,
I will fear no evil: for thou art with me. Psalm 23:4 (KJV)

Dear Ones,

The day will come when trial and tragedy will knock upon your door. The day will come when storms and strife will beat against your home. One day soon, you will go the way of all flesh, and breathe your last. Your heart will beat no more and your eyes will dim as earth and sky fade to black. God will summon you to Himself. A new day will dawn, brighter and more glorious than any this earth ever offered.

But until that day, through many valleys you must pass, the deepest and darkest being the valley in which you will encounter your own death. In these trivial times, we do all we can to avoid subjects such as suffering and death. Even Christians (especially Christians?) expect a life of comfort and ease. It seems many of us believe that though we might be disturbed by some minor turbulence now and then, death will dare to appear only with our permission—well after we have wrung all we can out of earthly life, filling our bucket of pleasures to the brim. Such an attitude, common as it is, is arrogant, foolish, and borderline blasphemous.

We would do much better to adopt the sobriety of Scripture, to view life and death as Christians of old did: Life is brief and death is soon. Such believers lived well...better than we do, more significantly in life, more triumphantly in death. They were not morbid;

they were balanced. They knew that fullness was not to be found here, but only with Christ in Paradise. Therefore, they were thankful for every pleasure given here below by their gracious God, and not surprised or unsettled by the expected bitter offerings of this fallen world.

Consider with me the saintly Puritan, John Owen (1616–1683). Owen is probably the greatest Christian mind England has ever produced. He preached to kings and parliaments, and was sought after by universities all over Europe and infant America. He knew the Lord and walked deeply with His God. But what many do not know is that he and his wife, Mary, had eleven children...ten of whom died in infancy. The one daughter that did survive to adulthood died of tuberculosis. Yet in his abundant writings, we find not *one* accusation toward God. There is a thankfulness for every mercy, and a continued and growing desire for purity of heart and life, even if produced through the deepest of tragedies. Hear him:

> What do we want? What would we be at? What do our souls desire? Is it not that we might have a more full, clear, stable comprehension of the wisdom, love, grace, goodness, holiness, righteousness, and power of God, as declared and exalted in Christ unto our redemption and eternal salvation?[34]

Can his be the same faith as ours? Such pure, heavenly desire sounds foreign to our earthbound ears.

Consider also a group of German theologians, followers of Jesus, who came together in 1653 to write up a "concise" definition of true Christianity. The resulting *Heidelberg Catechism* had 129 questions and answers (!), beginning with:

> "What is your only comfort in life and death?"
>
> The answer is:
>
> "That I am not my own, but belong—body and soul, in life and in death, to my faithful Savior Jesus Christ. He has fully paid for all my

sins with his precious blood, and has set me free from the tyranny of the devil. He also watches over me in such a way that not a hair can fall from my head without the will of my Father in heaven; in fact, all things must work together for my salvation. Because I belong to him, Christ, by His Holy Spirit, assures me of eternal life and makes me whole-heartedly willing and ready from now on to live for him."

Or ponder the words and witness of concentration camp survivor Corrie Ten Boom:

> This darkness is very deep, but our God has gone deeper still. When you have been to Calvary, even Ravensbrook looks small.[35]

Oh, my dear children, these men and women lived their brief, stormy lives well, and they died their certain deaths well. If you would do the same, then you must pray as the psalmist prayed:

> Teach us to number our days, that we may gain a heart of wisdom. (Psalm 90:12)

> Show me, Lord, my life's end and the number of my days; let me know how fleeting my life is. (Psalm 39:4)

These are not morbid prayers, they are realistic prayers. The writer is praying that he will not be flippant, arrogant, or foolish to think that death does not await him around every corner. Wisdom is gained when one faces up to the fact that life is stormy and brief.

> Why, you do not even know what will happen tomorrow. What is your life? You are a mist that appears for a little while and then vanishes. (James 4:14)
>
> The life of mortals is like grass, they flourish
> like a flower of the field;
> the wind blows over it and it is gone, and its place remembers it no more.

> But from everlasting to everlasting the Lord's love
> is with those who fear him, and his righteousness
> with their children's children—
>
> (Psalm 103:15-17)

It was short-lived Peter Marshall (1902-1949), chaplain of the US Senate, who said, "The measure of life is not its *duration* but its *donation.*" The even shorter-lived Jim Elliot (1927 -1956) said, "When it comes time to die, make sure that all you have to do is die." These men were not strange or unbalanced, but most of us are. Foolishly, we do not live our lives in the light of their certain end. God sends trials and tribulations to sober us, to focus us, to right us, but we fail to get the message and kick against His loving correction. They are meant to strip us of false hopes and cast us in our mortality upon the Lord, who grants life eternal:

> We do not want you to be uninformed, brothers and sisters, about the troubles we experienced in the province of Asia. We were under great pressure, far beyond our ability to endure, so that we despaired of life itself. Indeed, we felt we had received the sentence of death. But this happened that we might not rely on ourselves but on God, who raises the dead. (2 Corinthians 1:8, 9)

The glorious truth is that we have a Saviour who takes us through the storms of life and the great storm of death and judgment. Therefore, the Bible calls us to be people of faith, loving not our life more dearly than our Lord. There should be a sense of excitement, of anticipation at the thought of walking with Jesus through all things, good and bad, and finally being safely piloted through the tumult of death by Him who has been faithful in all things of life.

The words of Johan Rothe, translated by John Wesley, come to mind:

> Though waves and storms go o'er my head,
> Though strength, and health, and friends be gone,

Though joys be withered all and dead,
Though every comfort be withdrawn,
On this my steadfast soul relies,
Father, Thy mercy never dies.

Fixed on this ground will I remain,
Though my heart fail, and flesh decay;
This anchor shall my soul sustain,
When earth's foundations melt away;
Mercy's full power I then shall prove,
Loved with an everlasting love.

Oh, my dear children, I long for you to live lives rich with meaning and purpose! It is not my prayer that you will be secure in this life; rich, well padded, comfortable...and damned. It is not my prayer that all your dreams are fulfilled this side of eternity. I pray that your dreams will require Heaven. It is my prayer that yours will be lives of significance. Live every day in light of your final day. If you make it your holy aim to die well, you will find that you will live well. I am now fifty-six years old. Yes, I have hopes to one day be a little old man, my dear little old wife by my side, recounting the decades of God's faithfulness, with grandkids grown and flourishing before our eyes. But I have to tell you, I am ready to die. Not morbidly, not perversely, but realistically and expectantly. Jesus is my treasure and my shepherd, my goal, and my prize. Join with your mother and me in placing your treasure in Heaven and your whole hope in Christ, that one day you too may be able to say with Paul:

> For I am already being poured out like a drink offering, and the time for my departure is near. I have fought the good fight, I have finished the race, I have kept the faith. Now there is in store for me the crown of righteousness, which the Lord, the righteous Judge, will award to me on that day—and not only to me, but also to all who have longed for his appearing. (2 Timothy 4:6-8)

I first learned this hymn in Stoke-on-Trent, way back in 1983, at a funeral service. I thought it terribly morbid at first, but soon I came to see the strong theology and strengthening truth contained within it. Oh that we would think and sing such truths today:

****

Abide With Me

Abide with me; fast falls the eventide;
the darkness deepens; Lord, with me abide.
When other helpers fail and comforts flee,
Help of the helpless, O abide with me.

Swift to its close ebbs out life's little day;
earth's joys grow dim; its glories pass away;
Change and decay in all around I see;
O thou who changest not, abide with me.

I need thy presence every passing hour.
What but thy grace can foil the tempter's power?
Who, like thyself, my guide and stay can be?
Through cloud and sunshine, Lord, abide with me.

I fear no foe, with thee at hand to bless;
ills have no weight, and tears not bitterness.
Where is death's sting? Where, grave, thy victory?
I triumph still, if thou abide with me.

Hold thou thy cross before my closing eyes;
shine through the gloom and point me to the skies.
Heaven's morning breaks, and earth's vain shadows flee;
in life, in death, O Lord, abide with me.
(Henry F. Lyte, 1793-1847)

Letter 18

Behold Your Joy

I have told you this so that my joy may be in you and that your joy may be complete. John 15:11

Dear Children,

You will know that I have often struggled with melancholy. For some reason or reasons, I have had "gray" days, and even gray seasons. Usually it has been inexplicable; I have been unable to pinpoint a cause. Genetics? Physiology? The enemy? Circumstances? Some or all of the above? I really cannot say for sure. You have seen me battle depression, and as unpleasant as it has been for me, it has at times, I am sure, been equally unpleasant for you.

I do think that some are blessed with a more cheerful character than others. They seem to come out of the package that way. But I also believe that most, if not all bubbly people have their secret tears—perhaps not as many as others, but tears just the same. I would wish your mother's genes upon you over mine in this regard any day. She is such a steady character! I do not know what we would have done as a family, if she were like me in the depression department. Yet even she has had her gray days, when a mist rolls in and damp cold replaces warmth and light in her soul. Also, life brings its difficulties to the bright as well as to the melancholy. Tragedy strikes the bubbly and the bummed. Seasons of sadness are unavoidable this side of Heaven.

Over the past few years, God has been highlighting the theme of joy to me in the Bible. The word just keeps smiling at me. It has also sometimes rebuked me when I have chosen to be irritable and to wallow, rather than worship. Let me take you just a little way on my journey for joy, sharing with you some of the things I am learning. I trust this will strengthen and encourage your hearts, perhaps lead you to repent, and give you hope during those times when the fog won't seem to lift.

First, I am learning about the *nature* of God. God is eternally joyful. He is a community of joy: Father, Son, and Holy Spirit. The Bible tells of the "joy of the Lord" (Nehemiah 8:10), meaning, the joy the Lord possesses is an essential part of His nature and being.

At the centre of all creation is a Triune, joyful God. There is "joy in His presence" (Psalm 16:11; 21:6). "Strength and joy are in his dwelling place" (1 Chronicles 16:27). Certainly, He grieves over us as He interacts with our fallenness, but within Himself, He has never been depressed. He likes being God and would not want to be or do anything else. There has never been a bad mood, argument, or "funk" within the Trinity. God is an eternal community of joy.

Next, I am learning about the *heart* of God. If God were full of joy, but would not share His joy with His children, then we would have no hope of joy. But it is the heart of God to give us His joy.

Consider this: the Father has shared His limitless joy with the Son. (I am sure the Holy Spirit has received a good dose too!):

> You have loved righteousness and hated wickedness; therefore God, your God, has set you above your companions by anointing you with the oil of joy. (Hebrews 1:9)

So our Lord Jesus is full of joy divine. But Jesus cannot contain His joy, and desires to share it liberally with us. Don't take it from me, listen to Jesus:

> I have told you this so that my joy may be in you and that your joy may be complete. (John 15:11)

Now that settles the matter. And you need to receive God's heart towards you in this regard. Don't question the heart of God or doubt His desire to share His joy with you.

A.W. Tozer was absolutely right when he said that at the root of every issue is theological. Everything has to do with how we view God. A right knowledge of God will result in a cascade of truth into our lives. If you see God as a grim God, you will develop a perverse view which equates a sour mood and face with holiness. Understanding that God *is* joyful *and wants to share His joy with His children* is the key to joy!

I am learning that because God is joyful and wants to share His joy with me, His child, I must source all of my joy in Him and Him alone. For joy to be *in* me, it must be sourced *outside* of me. "The joy of the Lord is *your* strength," said Nehemiah to a weeping Jerusalem. The fact of God's joyfulness needs to become the wellspring of my strength and joy.

> Bring joy to your servant, Lord, for I put my trust in you. (Psalm 86:4)

How precious and powerful it is to look away from myself and my circumstances to the eternal, unchanging God as my source of joy. Kids, remember when you were young, and invariably the mood of the house was directly linked to the mood of your dad? If dad was happy, the house was happy. If dad was grumpy, the house was sad. That's just the way it was. (Sorry for my grumpy times! I repent!) So it is with life, on a grand scale. If God were not joyful, we could not be. But we can have joy today, no matter what trials and tribulations, chemical imbalances in the brain, or genetics may be in the way, because God is joyful in Himself, and our joy is to be rooted in His joy.

Finally, I have come to see that I must battle for joy. This may sound strange at first. But the point here is that joy often needs to be pursued when melancholy is the easier option. It takes no particular effort to be sour. A mud puddle of sorrow needs to be washed away in the river of God's essential happiness. This often means repenting. It is easier to slide down into Pilgrim's Slough of Despond than it is to look to the Lord, grab ourselves by the scruff of the neck, repent of joylessness, and refuse less than the will of Jesus for us.

It is always easier to wallow than to worship, to complain, to be irritable, to give in to the fleshly, perverse love of being the moping centre of attention. Growing in spiritual maturity for me has meant seeing grumpiness, in fact, seeing anything that robs me of Jesus' joy, as a sin. If Jesus wants to be my joy, to put His joy in me, and I would rather lust, be bitter, complain, or sit in the slough, then I am denying Jesus His heart for me.

It took me a long, long time—many years in fact—to see what was there for all to see in God's Word: God is a joyful God who has a heart to share His joy with His redeemed children. Don't wait as long as I did to behold Jesus, your joy.

William Cowper was a friend and follower of Jesus. A gifted poet, he lived a deeply troubled life. Following a childhood that scarred him psychologically, he battled serious depression for much of his life. But then, with the help of his dear friend, John Newton, this troubled soul learned to trust in the Lord and His mysterious ways of grace. Cowper wrote many hymns, but none of them has ministered to my soul or the souls of countless Christians like the following:

****

God Moves in a Mysterious Way

God moves in a mysterious way
His wonders to perform;
He plants His footsteps in the sea
And rides upon the storm.

Deep in unfathomable mines
Of never failing skill
He treasures up His bright designs
And works His sovereign will.

Ye fearful saints, fresh courage take;
The clouds ye so much dread
Are big with mercy and shall break
In blessings on your head.

Judge not the Lord by feeble sense,
But trust Him for His grace;
Behind a frowning providence
He hides a smiling face.

His purposes will ripen fast,
Unfolding every hour;
The bud may have a bitter taste,
But sweet will be the flower.

Blind unbelief is sure to err
And scan His work in vain;
God is His own interpreter,
And He will make it plain.
(William Cowper, 1731-1800)

Letter 19

Behold the God of the Impossible

Now to him who is able to do immeasurably more than all we ask or imagine, according to his power that is at work within us.
Ephesians 3:20

My Dearest Ones,

Upon William Borden's (1887-1913) gravestone in Cairo are written these words:

> Apart from faith in Christ there is no explanation
> for such a life.

Borden, a millionaire before twenty, gave up an easy life to follow Christ. Stirred by the needs of the world, the Yale graduate's motto for life was summed up in six words:

> No Reserves
> No Retreats
> No Regrets

Though he died young and unexpectedly of meningitis, his life stood as a testimony to his generation of what it means to treasure Christ supremely, to deny all for Him, to trust all to Him, and to live this brief, valuable life in view of eternity. Thus, he stirred a generation to renewed missionary endeavour.

I am struck by those words on his simple gravestone. I want that to be said of my life, too. I want to live a life that cannot be explained apart from faith in the faithfulness of Christ. I want to live a life in which either Jesus comes through, or all is disaster. I do not want the safe option.

I want to live an impossible life—to the glory of God.

I want the same for each of you.

Jesus calls people to do the impossible. His very call has within it the power to respond. He tells a lame man to walk, and he does. He bids a crippled hand to be stretched forth, and it is. He summons a dead girl to get up, and she rises. These are all impossible scenes. But they are pictures of what Jesus does:

> He speaks, and, listening to His voice,
> New life the dead receive,
> The mournful, broken hearts rejoice,
> The humble poor believe.
>
> Hear Him, ye deaf; His praise, ye dumb,
> Your loosened tongues employ;
> Ye blind, behold your Savior come,
> And leap, ye lame, for joy
> (Charles Wesley)

Impossibilities, every one!

Children, *we* are not amazing. This life is not about our strength, or what we can naturally do. Jesus does the impossible through surrendered lives. This is not always expressed or seen in a big ministry or in other obvious ways. The mother that sacrifices every day to pour herself out for and into her children is a living testimony to God's power. The teenager that swims upstream, against the current of his peers in order to follow Christ, is living the impossible life of faith. The man that pursues holiness of heart and life against the pull and powers of the world, his own flesh, and Satan himself, is truly a miracle man. The person that lives by principles before interests lives on the heights with Christ.[36]

Jesus is calling us to live a life we could never live without Him: A life of holiness, faithfulness, constancy, sacrifice, and joyfulness. We may never see the full ramifications of such a life, but you can be sure that its impact will be more far-reaching than anyone could ever imagine.

John Bunyan (1628-1688) lived an impossible life, although most of his friends and neighbours would not have noticed it. Only history has revealed it. He was a "tinker," that is, a maker of pots and pans. Poor and poorly educated, one would never expect God's power to be displayed in such a life. When he was thirty, his wife died, leaving him with four children, one of whom was blind. He remarried, and he and Elizabeth had two more children before Bunyan was imprisoned for the crime of preaching as a "nonconformist." All he had to do was agree not to preach, yet he said to the magistrates, "If you release me today, I shall preach tomorrow!"[37] Think of Elizabeth, alone with the children. The magistrates asked her to pressure John to give up preaching. She refused to aid them. John Piper gives the text of her dialogue with the magistrates in full. I reproduce in part it here:

> Now she met with one stiff question:
>
> "Would he stop preaching?"
>
> "My lord, he dares not leave off preaching as long as he can speak."
>
> "He preacheth nothing but the word of God!" she says.
>
> Mr. Twisden, in a rage: "He runneth up and down and doeth harm."
>
> "No, my lord, it is not so; God hath owned him and done much good by him."
>
> The angry man: "His doctrine is the doctrine of the devil."

She: "My lord, when the righteous Judge shall appear, it will be
known that his doctrine is not the doctrine of the devil!"

Bunyan's biographer comments, "Elizabeth Bunyan was simply an
English peasant woman: could she have spoken with more dignity
had she been a crowned queen?"[38]

In the twelve years he spent imprisoned, he produced shoelaces to
sell to try to meet the needs of his family. And, oh yes, I almost forgot,
he also produced a book, *The Pilgrim's Progress*. This remarkable
book is arguably the *second* best-selling book of all time, next to the
Bible, which makes John Bunyan, the humble tinker from Bedford,
the *best-selling author of all time*.

Impossible? Not with Jesus.

Do not ask God for an easier life; ask Him to display His power in
the life that He has given to you. Do hard things. Make right choices
no matter what. Trust Jesus for the miraculous outcome. Jesus is the
Lord of the impossible.

I first heard the ancient hymn of Bunyan's below when pastoring
in Cornwall. At a missions conference we were holding at our church
in Looe, Cornwall, Bob and Dee Molton had this sung prior to their
departure to serve Jesus overseas. It elicits visions of Pilgrim on his
brave journey towards the Celestial City, and so stirs my heart!

****

He Who Would Valiant Be

He who would valiant be 'gainst all disaster,

Let him in constancy follow the Master.

There's no discouragement shall make him once relent

His first avowed intent to be a pilgrim.

Who so beset him round with dismal stories
Do but themselves confound—his strength the more is.
No foes shall stay his might; though he with giants fight,
He will make good his right to be a pilgrim.

Hobgoblin nor foul fiend can daunt his spirit,
He knows he at the end shall life inherit.
Then fancies fly away, He'll fear not what men say,
He'll labor night and day To be a pilgrim.
(John Bunyan, 1628-1688)

Letter 20

Behold the Lord, Your Righteousness

This is his name whereby he shall be called, The Lord Our Righteousness. Jeremiah 23:6 (KJV)

My Dear Children,

Martin Luther did not get everything right, but he did get the main thing right. He discovered in the Bible the wondrous truth of God, that in the Gospel we are made right with a Holy God, not through anything we do, but through the work of Christ on our behalf. Christ takes away our sin and gives us in its stead His righteousness.

Luther had a friend, a friar named George. To him he wrote these moving words:

> I should be very glad to know what is the state of your soul. Is it not tired of its own righteousness? Does it not breathe freely at last, and does it not confide in the righteousness of Christ? In our days, pride seduces many, and especially those who labor with all their might to become righteous. Not understanding the righteousness of God that is given to us freely in Christ Jesus, they wish to stand before Him on their own merits. But that cannot be. When you were living with me, you were in that error, and so was I. I am yet struggling unceasingly against it, and I have not yet entirely triumphed over it.
>
> Oh, my dear brother, learn to know Christ, and him crucified. Learn to sing unto him a new song, to despair of yourself, and to say to him: Thou, Lord Jesus Christ, art my righteousness, and I am thy sin. Thou hast taken what was mine, and hast given me what was thine. What thou wast not, thou didst become, in order that I might become what I was not!–Beware, my dear George, of pretending to such purity as

no longer to confess yourself a sinner: for Christ dwells only with
sinners. He came down from heaven, where he was living among
the righteous, in order to live also among sinners. Meditate carefully
upon this love of Christ, and you will taste all its unspeakable conso-
lation. If our labors and afflictions could give peace to the conscience,
why should Christ have died? You will not find peace, save in him, by
despairing of yourself and of your works, and in learning with what
love he opens his arms to you, taking all your sins upon himself, and
giving thee all his righteousness.[39]

In those words is summed up the wonder of the Gospel. Jesus
takes our sin and credits to us His righteousness. I do not fully
understand the depth of this (though I have followed Jesus nearly
forty years and delighted to make a life's study of the wonders of
our salvation). I marvel more than I understand. I know this much:
People the world over, especially religious people, and certainly
many who would call themselves evangelical Christians, labour to
produce their own righteousness, hoping thereby to please God. This
is the natural bent of every fallen creature. Oh, the intolerable burden
of religion! It is capable of producing only two things: 1) Pride, as
one feels himself doing better than others or, 2) Despair, as one sees
his situation as hopeless.

The Gospel comes with the startling, shocking, *scandalous*[40] declaration that:

> He (God the Father) made Him who knew no sin (Jesus, God the
> Son) to be sin on our behalf, so that we might become the righteous-
> ness of God in Him.
> (2 Corinthians 5:21)

The Gospel delivers us from a performance-based religion (Have
I fasted enough? Repented enough? Read my Bible enough?), to confidence in Christ, to a faith which looks *away* from itself (*outside* of
itself), to Jesus for righteousness. Here is at last a righteous man.

Tempted in every way, as we are, yet without sin. The Bible teaches us that through faith in Christ, despairing of our own righteousness, God enfolds us in the righteousness of Christ.

Providing righteousness for us is something God has done through His Son. Sin has so tainted every aspect of us (this is what "total depravity" means), we are incapable of producing the righteousness that God requires. So God, in His unsurpassable wisdom and grace, provides righteousness for us through Jesus.

> But whatever were gains to me I now consider loss for the sake of Christ. What is more, I consider everything a loss because of the surpassing worth of knowing Christ Jesus my Lord, for whose sake I have lost all things. I consider them garbage, that I may gain Christ and be found in him, not having a righteousness of my own that comes from the law, but that which is through faith in Christ—the righteousness that comes from God on the basis of faith.
> (Philippians 3:7-9)

Never was a man more earnest to be right with God than George Whitefield (1714-1770). An ordained minister in the Church of England, he subjected himself to the strictest religious life, almost killing himself with fasting:

> I began to fast twice a week for thirty-six hours together, prayed many times a day, and received the sacrament every Lord's Day. I fasted myself almost to death all the forty days of Lent, during which I made it a point of duty never to go less than three times a day to public worship, besides seven times a day to private prayers. Yet I knew no more that I was to be born a new creature in Christ Jesus than if I had never been born at all.[41]

When near death from his "religion," someone gave him Henry Scougal's book, *The Life of God in the Soul of Man*. Of reading this book, Whitefield writes:

God soon showed me..."that true religion was a union of the soul with God, and Christ formed within us," a ray of divine light was instantaneously darted in upon my soul.[42]

Whitefield later wrote:

God was pleased to remove the heavy load (of performance-based religiosity), to enable me to lay hold of his dear Son by a living faith. With what joy-joy unspeakable-was my soul filled! (parenthesis added)[43]

The Gospel tells us we are "justified," that is, declared right before God, by the gift of God's grace, which we receive by faith alone. *Christ takes our sin and gives us His righteousness.* This is the heart of the Gospel. I once had a dear friend who, after suffering a great failure in his Christian ministry, told me: "The doctrine of justification by grace through faith kept me from committing suicide." The fact that he, regardless of his failure, stood justified before his God, his sin removed and robed in the righteousness of Christ, his Saviour, was his sufficient hope in the midst of despair.

I want you to see that the Gospel involves more than the forgiveness of sin. It is not just that God wipes the slate clean through the death of Christ for our sins. He then writes on that slate, "righteous in Christ." And He writes this not in chalk, but indelible ink. Imagine you were in deep debt, only to find that a man of great wealth and grace had paid it off completely—moreover, he had credited his great wealth to your account. The wonder of the Gospel is that God has done this for you. To ignore the righteousness that God freely supplies, and endeavour to produce your own, is not only futile but offensive to God, because it supposes you can outdo His goodness with your own.

You can try until you exhaust yourself to serve up your own righteousness, but you never will. You can look inside yourself all your life in search of a righteous heart of your own making, but you will never find one. Or, you can trust Christ, looking away from yourself, to Him who invites you to find your righteousness in Him, breathing deeply of the pure, fresh air of the Gospel. The freedom for the Christian comes when he gives up and confides in Christ alone, and His righteousness.

> It is because of him that you are in Christ Jesus, who has become for us wisdom from God—that is, our righteousness, holiness and redemption. (1 Corinthians 1:30)

The hymn below, written by the remarkable Nikolaus von Zinzendorf of the Moravians, became a favourite of John Wesley, who translated it from the original German to English. Do not rush through it, but take time and meditate upon the truth that it brings. It will be a blessing to your soul:

****

Jesus, Thy Blood and Righteousness

> Jesus, Thy blood and righteousness
> My beauty are, my glorious dress;
> 'Midst flaming worlds, in these arrayed,
> With joy shall I lift up my head.
>
> Bold shall I stand in Thy great day;
> For who aught to my charge shall lay?
> Fully absolved through these I am
> From sin and fear, from guilt and shame.
>
> The holy, meek, unspotted Lamb,
> Who from the Father's bosom came,
> Who died for me, e'en me to atone,
> Now for my Lord and God I own.

Lord, I believe Thy precious blood,
Which, at the mercy seat of God,
Forever doth for sinners plead,
For me, e'en for my soul, was shed.

Lord, I believe were sinners more
Than sands upon the ocean shore,
Thou hast for all a ransom paid,
For all a full atonement made.

When from the dust of death I rise
To claim my mansion in the skies,
Ev'n then this shall be all my plea,
Jesus hath lived, hath died, for me.

This spotless robe the same appears,
When ruined nature sinks in years;
No age can change its glorious hue,
The robe of Christ is ever new.

Jesus, the endless praise to Thee,
Whose boundless mercy hath for me—
For me a full atonement made,
An everlasting ransom paid.

O let the dead now hear Thy voice;
Now bid Thy banished ones rejoice;
Their beauty this, their glorious dress,
Jesus, Thy blood and righteousness.
(Count Nikolaus L. von Zinzendorf, 1700-1760)

Letter 21

Behold Him Who Has Defeated Your Adversary

Now the prince of this world will be driven out. John 12:31

My Children,

Should you determine to live a life of meaning and purpose (and I hope that you do), choosing Christ and His Kingdom as your supreme treasure, determining by faith to live a life of love and service, then you will find that you have a very real adversary. There is an enemy, a foe pitted against you.

C.S. Lewis was right when he said that if when we think of the Devil, we imagine someone in red tights, then he has already won. He is far more real than that.

The Bible calls him:

The Enemy

The Accuser

The Father of Lies

The Prince of Darkness

The Thief

A Roaring Lion

The Serpent

An Angel of Light

Certainly, he is real—a prideful, fallen angel who knows his doom is sealed and is now determined to take as many down to the pit with him as he can. To do so, he does not have to make you into a witch. He is very happy if he can simply get your focus off of Christ and onto anything else. Satan will be equally glad to make you "super-spiritual" or adulterous. Either one will do. Both will ruin you and bring shame to Christ and His cause. He managed to produce both in the Corinthian Church:

> **Super-Spirituality:** But I am afraid that, as the serpent deceived Eve by his craftiness, your minds will be led astray from the simplicity and purity of *devotion* to Christ. (2 Corinthians 11:3, NASB)
>
> **Gross·Immorality:** It is actually reported that·there is immorality among you, and immorality of such a kind as does not exist even among the Gentiles, that someone has his father's wife. And you are proud! (1 Corinthians 5:1, 2, NASB)

Now Satan has been soundly defeated in the crucifixion and resurrection of Jesus. He knows that. When Jesus Christ absorbed the wrath of God for us, bearing our guilt and pollution, dying a sinner's death, only to rise again in victory, the Bible teaches us that Satan was defeated, then and there.

> And having disarmed the powers.and authorities, he made a public spectacle of them, triumphing over them by the cross. (Colossians 2:15)

He has been defanged. Certainly he is bigger than *us*, and dangerous enough to do *us* harm. But he is nothing in comparison to Jesus. Therefore, Satan no longer need have any hold upon the one who is hidden in Christ and careful to follow closely after his Shepherd.

As a father, I am often especially aware of Satan's sinister approaches.in attacking our family. He used and uses no end of subtle and not so subtle measures to try and destroy our unity, joy, and witness. Your mom and I prayed and prayed over our lives and home, trusting in the Lord Jesus to protect us; but also being careful not to give Satan a way in through graceless religion, bitterness and unforgiveness, immoral behavior, or spiritual pride. Oh, his ways are so sinister and slippery!

I found that the greatest weapon we have against Satan is to constantly make much of Jesus and His Gospel, to ourselves, and to one another:

> They triumphed over him by the blood of the lamb and by the word of their testimony. (Revelation 12:11)

Keeping Christ central, forgiveness at the fore, glorying in the Gospel of Grace, refusing to hold something against another, speaking often of the goodness of God—all these are powerful spiritual weapons! Cultivating a thankful heart, walking in the spirit opposite from what the flesh desires, keeping it simple with the Lord, honouring one another above ourselves, believing and behaving the Word— Satan cannot abide such basic Christianity!

If you are foolish enough to flirt with sin, you will find that you are giving a foothold to the devil. This adversary will certainly do damage to you and yours. He can spoil entire families, churches, and ministries, and he loves the very process. Look, if you are going to live foolishly and carelessly, not guarding your heart, taking your eyes off the Lord, and if you are going to toy with sin and temptation, Satan will have you for lunch. He will ruin your testimony, rob your joy, hurt those who love you, and do a victory dance on your broken life.

Equally (and this may be a more likely device he tries on some of you), if you are going to forget the wonders of the Gospel and become "super-spiritual" and weird, you will make the devil's day. True Christianity never moves away from a simple trust in Christ and the Gospel. It remains fixed upon the Bible as sure and sufficient. Satan often strategizes to get a zealous believer sidetracked into "deeper things" which may be, in reality, bogs and ditches.

He may now be toothless, but he can still do a lot of damage with those gums! It does not have to happen. Our slimy, drooling foe does not have to have his way with us. Our Lord Jesus outdid Satan at every turn when He walked this earth, "tempted in every way...yet he did not sin" (Hebrews 4:15). Again, He scored the decisive victory at the cross and empty tomb. The outcome is decided. Our victory over the enemy is founded in Christ's triumph. It is as we abide in Him, and keep a thankful, obedient, believing heart that we give that thief no opportunity for entry.

I know that some of our friends profess a "deliverance" ministry. I am certainly not about to say there are not times when a devilish intruder needs to be forcibly evicted. Jesus certainly did this, as did Paul. But, I also think the devil loves nothing better than a hullabaloo being made over him. Bullies love attention, and sometimes the least said, the better.

In my experience, the Prince of Darkness cannot abide the Light of the World; the Father of Lies cannot abide the Lord of Truth; the Roaring Lion cannot abide the Good Shepherd; the Accuser of the Brethren cannot abide the Friend of Sinners. In other words, ministering Jesus in all His wonderful aspects to yourself and others is just more than Satan can handle. If you want to defeat your dark foe, *make much of Jesus.* The simple, Christ-exalting Gospel is the most powerful spiritual weapon of all.

Martin Luther certainly aimed a mighty missile at Satan and his hellish hordes when he rediscovered the true and simple Gospel. In so doing, he set himself up for no end of very real satanic attack.[44] But he learned to take refuge in his Saviour and the cross. In Christ, this weak and often attacked man lived a life of triumph over the enemy of his soul.

I love Luther's hymn, "A Mighty Fortress Is Our God," because being rich in Christian truth, it was written out of the real-life experience of battle and victory in that little man's great big life:

****

A Mighty Fortress Is Our God

A mighty fortress is our God, a bulwark never failing;
Our helper He, amid the flood of mortal ills prevailing:
For still our ancient foe doth seek to work us woe;
His craft and power are great, and, armed with cruel hate,
On earth is not his equal.

Did we in our own strength confide, our striving would be losing;
Were not the right Man on our side, the Man of God's own choosing:
Dost ask who that may be? Christ Jesus, it is He;
Lord Sabaoth, His Name, from age to age the same,
And He must win the battle.

And though this world, with devils filled, should threaten to undo us,
We will not fear, for God hath willed His truth to triumph through us:
The Prince of Darkness grim, we tremble not for him;
His rage we can endure, for lo, his doom is sure,
One little word shall fell him.

That word above all earthly powers, no thanks to them, abideth;
The Spirit and the gifts are ours through Him Who with us sideth:
Let goods and kindred go, this mortal life also;
The body they may kill: God's truth abideth still,
His kingdom is forever.
(Martin Luther, 1483-1546)

Letter 22

Behold Your Coming King

"Yes, I am coming soon." Amen. Come, Lord Jesus. Revelation 22:20

My Children,

Those who live in sure hope for the future accomplish the most in the present. Some would say that those living in the expectant hope of the return of Jesus, with His Kingdom coming in fullness, are too starry-eyed to be of any earthly good. They do not know their Bibles or Christian history.

Lord Shaftesbury, Antony Ashley Cooper, lived from 1801-1885. He is yet another hero of mine! Born into a wealthy and powerful family as the "7th Earl of Shaftesbury," he was a committed follower of Jesus by the time he became a member of Parliament in 1826 (just twenty-five years old!). For the rest of his life, Shaftesbury worked tirelessly for the broken in society. He was a voice for the voiceless, and a strong man for the weak man.

Rightly dubbed, "The Poor Man's Earl," Shaftesbury, a father of ten, laboured against his times to see countless reforms in what was the brutal Dickensian world of 19th century Britain. He was the driving force behind reforms in the "lunacy laws" (seeking humane treatment of the insane), child labour and "chimney sweep" laws, mining regulations, education statutes for the poor, and in many other areas of social ill. This Christian man, along with William and Catherine Booth, Robert Raikes, William Wilberforce, and other motivated followers of Jesus, changed the moral and social climate of their generation, and of ours.

Loved by the poor, when Lord Shaftesbury died in October 1885, "The streets along the route from Grosvenor Square and Westminster

Abbey were thronged with poor people, costermongers, flower-girls, boot-blacks, crossing-sweepers, factory-hands and similar workers who waited for hours to see Shaftesbury's coffin as it passed by."[45]

It is generally unknown that this great and humble servant of the poor was motivated by the continual thought that Jesus would soon return. Lord Shaftesbury lived in the hope and expectation of the real, visible, imminent return of his Lord and Saviour, and this was a constant motive for his tireless service. Near the end of his rich and useful life he said,

> In the last 40 years, I do not believe that I have had one conscious thought that did not include the idea of the return of Jesus Christ.[46]

I remember reading that every time he heard the clock strike, he prayed for Christ to come again.

Most of us are far too earthbound. Lord Shaftesbury had an uncommon, but *normal* view of things. His eyes were directed towards the skies, even as they scrutinized the urgent needs of earth.

Here is what the Bible teaches, in brief:

Jesus will come again—suddenly, visibly, physically, and triumphantly. History as we have known it will then come to a close. The age of mission and evangelism will end. This age of tears, trials, death and sin will be over. Satan and his swarm will be condemned forever, along with all who loved wickedness. Christ's Kingdom will begin in fullness and we will know, love, serve, and enjoy the Lord and each other in unimaginable glory.

I could say so much more, but my purpose now is to encourage you that this future fact is intended by Jesus to be a source of present purpose. Hear Him:

> But about that day or hour no one knows, not even the angels in heaven, nor the Son, but only the Father. Be on guard! Be alert! You do not know when that time will come. It's like a man going away: he leaves his house and puts his servants in charge, each with their assigned task, and tells the one at the door to keep watch.

Therefore keep watch because you do not know when the owner of the house will come back–whether in the evening, or at midnight, or when the rooster crows, or at dawn. If he comes suddenly, do not let him find you sleeping. What I say to you, I say to everyone: "Watch!" (Mark 13:32-36)

Hear the Apostle Paul:

Therefore, my dear brothers and sisters (in view of the appearing of Christ and the resurrection of our bodies), stand firm. Let nothing move you. Always give yourselves fully to the work of the Lord, because you know that your labor in the Lord is not in vain. (1 Corinthians 15:58)

I know that plenty of Christians have their particular views of just how things will pan out. I don't. Whole denominations and movements have been established over millennial theories. Followers of Jesus fight over this! I won't. I just keep it simple: Jesus is coming back and it could be today. Or, I could be summoned home today, and I don't want to be in the wrong place doing the wrong thing when my Boss turns up. I want to be found doing what He told me to do: To quote a great servant of the Lord, "Praising the Lord, and fighting the devil."[47]

A.W. Tozer (whose writings were vital to my spiritual formation) was right on when he proposed that we are lukewarm about Jesus' return because we have it so good these days. However, Christians through most of history, and many Christians today in other lands, long for Jesus to rip apart the skies and usher in a new day. If we loved Him as much as we claim to, we would labour and pray as did "The Poor Man's Earl" for our Beloved to come over the mountains and gather His Bride in His arms.

I do not mean to be morbid in the least when I say that taken as a whole, the New Testament presents a long life as the *third best* thing a follower of Jesus can experience. The first, without question, is to see Jesus come back soon, while we are busy with our hands to the plough. The next is to serve Him with all our might, but soon depart this life and be with Him. The third is to live a long life, serving His purposes, and then to finally go to be with the Church Triumphant, in the very presence of the Lord. Don't take my word for this, check it out with your Bible and I think you will see I am right.[48]

The final cry of the New Testament should be the constant cry of the follower of the Lamb. My child, it is my deepest prayer that it be the true cry of your Godward heart:

Maranatha! *Even so come, Lord Jesus.*

****

For All the Saints

For all the saints, who from their labors rest,
who thee by faith before the world confessed,
thy name, O Jesus, be forever blest.
Alleluia, Alleluia!

Thou wast their rock, their fortress, and their might;
thou Lord, their captain in the well-fought fight;
thou in the darkness drear, their one true light.
Alleluia, Alleluia!

O may thy soldiers, faithful, true, and bold,
fight as the saints who nobly fought of old,
and win with them the victor's crown of gold.
Alleluia, Alleluia!

O blest communion, fellowship divine!
We feebly struggle, they in glory shine;

yet all are one in thee, for all are thine.
Alleluia, Alleluia!

And when the strife is fierce, the warfare long,
steals on the ear the distant triumph song,
and hearts are brave again, and arms are strong.
Alleluia, Alleluia!

From earth's wide bounds, from ocean's farthest coast,
through gates of pearl streams in the countless host,
singing to Father, Son, and Holy Ghost:
Alleluia, Alleluia!
(William W. How, 1823-1897)

Letter 23

Behold Your Reward

The kingdom of heaven is like treasure hidden in a field. When a man found it, he hid it again, and then in his joy went and sold all he had and bought that field. Matthew 13:44

Dear Ones,

Here is a history exam for you: Who was the first man to walk on the moon? If you rightly say Neil Armstrong, you really do not deserve a prize. The second? Small prize for knowing it was Buzz Aldrin. Okay, big prize for this right answer: What was the name of the third astronaut on that first lunar mission? I mean the one who did not get to land on the moon, but had to orbit in the command module for twenty-two lonely hours while Neil and Buzz got all the glory of being the first men to walk on another heavenly body. I bet you cannot remember.

Michael Collins was the unsung hero of that mission. While his two soon to be household name colleagues bounced around 30,000 feet below, on the surface of the moon, Collins' job was to keep the ship that would return them to earth ready to receive them. With each distant orbit, as Collins passed around the dark side of the moon, he was truly the loneliest man in the universe, farther from Earth than ever a man has been.

The unsung hero did his job perfectly. When Armstrong and Aldrin lifted off the moon's surface, Collins was there to meet them in the sky, dock with them, and whisk them home to the good Earth. I have often thought about Collins. He clearly drew the short straw on that trip. But he played his part while others got the glory.

That just happens to be how the Kingdom of God works. This is a kingdom of unsung heroes. A few are famous, most of us are not. John the Baptist said it well when Jesus' crowds were growing at the expense of his: "A person can receive (in terms of fame, ministry, influence) only what is given to him from heaven" (John 3:27).

If you are looking for a near and earthly reward, following Jesus is sure to disappoint. If you are looking for *any* reward (other than one in particular), you are sure to feel let down by Christianity. Others may get a reward of fame, accolade, or finance, while you are somewhere playing your part on the dark side of the moon where no one can see you, save the one who sees everything.

Yet there is a reward for the follower of Jesus that far outweighs all others. The reward is none other, and nothing less, than Jesus Christ Himself. *He* is the treasure we get. God motivates us by the promise of a reward. Remember, when the Bible speaks of "rewards" for the believer (and it does), it cannot be speaking of the carnal rewards that the sons of the earth receive in abundance: cars, money, or creature comforts. There can only be one *true* reward for the lover of Jesus, and this can only be Jesus Himself. Anything and everything else would be a letdown. Hence, when the Bible says that God "rewards those who earnestly seek him" (Hebrews 11:6), the only reward for one who is diligently seeking Jesus *must* be Jesus.

Think about it, if you are diligently seeking your TV remote, and find instead your other black sock, this find does not and cannot satisfy you, for it was not the object of your search. The reward for one who is earnestly seeking Jesus cannot be money, cars, or homes. Jesus is not the means to some other end, but is the end, Himself.[49]

So the Kingdom is likened to a man who finds a treasure that becomes more valuable than all other possessions combined: "In his joy he went and sold all he had and bought that treasure." There is nothing begrudging about this exchange. It is a *joy* for the man to rid himself of everything else and gain a field with treasure. Others may consider him crazy, but he knows better. The search is over. The treasure has been found, the reward is secure.

The psalmist was almost ruined as he envied the temporal rewards of the godless. Their lives seemed so easy, their rewards so immediate, and there he was, on the dark side of the moon! But then he considered all things in the light of eternity. Their present rewards were temporary, and their godless doom was sure. His reward, though now unseen, was safe, a treasure undefiled, kept in Heaven for him. His near ruin became a deep rejoicing:

> Yet I am always with you;
> you hold me by my right hand.
>
> You guide me with your counsel,
> and afterward you will take me into glory.
>
> Whom have I in heaven but you?
> And earth has nothing I desire besides you.
>
> My flesh and my heart may fail,
> but God is the strength of my heart
> and my portion forever. (Psalm 73:23-26)

How I love these words! Surely they must speak of the purest "religion" anywhere to be found. My dear children, you will find that when Jesus becomes all that you want, then you shall have Jesus in ever-increasing fullness. Only then shall He be to you your reward and your treasure. It is my continued prayer for you that every lesser love will dissatisfy (even the good and right loves of family and friends), until you will seek and find your heart's reward in Christ Himself.

Unsung hero you may be, but unspeakably precious to the Lord Jesus. Let Him be your reward both now and forever, and you will be the possessor of more true wealth than all the world could ever offer.

> For to me, to live is Christ and to die is gain.
> (Philippians 1:21)

I love the hymn below by Rhea Miller, which has just recently come my way. Every time I sing it, these words re-centre my soul upon Christ, my treasure and reward:

****

I'd Rather Have Jesus

I'd rather have Jesus than silver or gold;
I'd rather be His than have riches untold;
I'd rather have Jesus than houses or lands;
I'd rather be led by His nail-pierced hand

Than to be the king of a vast domain
And be held in sin's dread sway;
I'd rather have Jesus than anything
This world affords today.

I'd rather have Jesus than men's applause;
I'd rather be faithful to His dear cause;
I'd rather have Jesus than worldwide fame;
I'd rather be true to His holy name

He's fairer than lilies of rarest bloom;
He's sweeter than honey from out the comb;
He's all that my hungering spirit needs;
I'd rather have Jesus and let Him lead

Than to be the king of a vast domain
And be held in sin's dread sway;
I'd rather have Jesus than anything
This world affords today.
(Rhea F. Miller, 1894-1966)

Letter 24

Behold Him Who Carries Your Pain

Surely he took up our pain and bore our suffering. Isaiah 53:4

My Dear Children,

In 1858, John G. Paton and his newlywed bride, Mary, set sail from Scotland bound for the cannibal island of Tanna, in the New Hebrides. Soon after arriving, they were blessed with the birth of a son. Their first anniversary was to be their last, as Mary died of a tropical fever on March 3, 1859. Before the month was out, their infant son joined his mother in the grave. Alone on a cannibal island on the other side of the world, Patton wrote, "But for Jesus...I'd have gone mad and died beside that lonely grave."[50]

In time, John would remarry while on a visit to Australia. He and Maggie would have ten children, four of whom would die in infancy. They ministered on the island of Aniwa in the New Hebrides...for 33 years. "John G. learned the language and reduced it to writing. Maggie taught a class of about fifty women and girls who became experts at sewing, singing and plaiting hats, and reading. They trained the teachers, translated and printed and expounded the Scriptures, ministered to the sick and dying, dispensed medicines every day, taught them the use of tools, held worship services every Lord's Day and sent native teachers to all the villages to preach the gospel."[51]

Enduring many years of deprivation, danger from natives and disease, they continued with their work, and after many years of patient ministry, the entire island of Aniwa professed Christianity. In 1899, Paton saw his Aniwa New Testament printed and the establishment of missionaries on twenty-five of the thirty islands of the New Hebrides.

Now, I have to ask, "How does someone *do* that?" How does a man *endure* in the face of such *pain*? How does a couple *keep going* after four of their children die in some dark foreign land?

The secret is found in the words of Paton's journal from 1859, "Apart from Jesus..." This is the key, the open secret to the life of faith that endures and emerges victorious from the veil of tears. Jesus Christ is famous for being our *sin* bearer, but did you know that He is also our *sadness* bearer? "Surely he hath borne our griefs, and carried our sorrows..." (Isaiah 53:4, KJV), "...a man of sorrows, and acquainted with grief..." (Isaiah 53:3, KJV). Jesus is the God who invites the weak, pained, and broken to *Himself*: "Come to me, all you who are weary and burdened, and I will give you rest" (Matthew 11:28). He does not subcontract out His personal concern to a mere archangel, but delights to take upon Himself our griefs and sorrows: "Cast all your anxiety on him because he cares for you" (1 Peter 5:7).

It is a reality that must be reckoned with, that *this* life is filled with pain. Jesus wants to carry our pain. I can imagine that John Paton did just what countless other simple saints have done for thousands of years. He literally *gave his pain to Jesus.* What else could he do? Well, in fact he could have done two other things: 1) Kept it to himself, stuffing it way down deep inside until it poisoned his very soul, or; 2) Taken it out on others, in anger, moroseness, or hardness until it poisoned all those around him. You and I have these same three options every time pain is our unwelcome companion: Keep it, take it out on others, or give it to Jesus.

Just consider this God we serve! What a Saviour! He takes not only our sin but our sadness upon Himself, giving us joy where sadness once was:

> The Spirit of the Sovereign Lord is on me,
>
> because the Lord has anointed me
>
> to proclaim good news to the poor.
>
> He has sent me to bind up the brokenhearted,
>
> to proclaim freedom for the captives

and release from darkness for the prisoners,
to proclaim the year of the Lord's favor
and the day of vengeance of our God,

To comfort all who mourn,
and provide for those who grieve in Zion—
to bestow on them a crown of beauty
instead of ashes,
the oil of joy
instead of mourning,
and a garment of praise
instead of a spirit of despair.

They will be called oaks of righteousness,
a planting of the Lord
for the display of his splendour. (Isaiah 61:1-3)

Beauty for ashes, gladness for mourning, praise for despair, broken people becoming strong as oaks, all for the display of *His* splendour! Jesus is made famous when He takes pain and gives joy!

So often, I have made a broken trip to my Saviour's side, to unload my hurting heart. And He has greeted me time and again with no rebuke, but I have heard His voice in my spirit saying: "Why have you been so long in coming? I would have received you sooner and taken this burden away. You carried it too long! It almost broke you and those around you. I am happy to take it now, and if you need to come again, do so quickly."

Dear ones, if you will survive in ministry for the long haul, then you must learn now that our Jesus is our caring God who invites us to come with offerings of need and brokenness. Truly, He is the "lover of our souls." Keep your "pain account" short. Give your pain to the Lord Jesus as often as you detect hurt in your heart.

H.G. Spafford discovered this wondrous truth about our Jesus Christ, through almost unimaginable heartbreak. A follower of Jesus and an influential Chicago lawyer, his pains began to multiply in 1870, when he and his wife endured the death of their only son, aged four. The next year, the Great Chicago Fire destroyed almost all of his considerable real estate holdings.

> Two years later, in 1873, Spafford decided his family should take a holiday somewhere in Europe, and chose England, knowing that his friend D.L. Moody would be preaching there in the fall. He was delayed because of business, so he sent his family ahead: his wife, Anna, and their four daughters, eleven-year-old Anna "Annie," nine-year-old Margaret Lee, five-year-old Elizabeth "Bessie," and two-year-old Tanetta.
>
> On November 22, 1873, while crossing the Atlantic on the steamship *Ville du Harve*, the ship was struck by an iron sailing vessel and 226 people lost their lives, including all four of Spafford's daughters. Anna Spafford survived the tragedy. Upon arriving in England, she sent a telegram to Spafford beginning "Saved alone."
>
> Spafford then sailed to England, going over the location of his daughters' deaths. According to Bertha Spafford Vester, a daughter born after the tragedy, Spafford wrote 'It is Well with My Soul' on this journey.[52]

Here is one of my most loved hymns, so rich in meaning, for it was born out of the real-life experience of pain given to Christ. It tells the soul to find its solace in the Gospel, that Christ's peace might flood in to possess the troubled heart:

****

It Is Well with My Soul

When peace, like a river, attendeth my way,
When sorrows like sea billows roll;
Whatever my lot, Thou has taught me to say,
It is well, it is well, with my soul.

It is well, with my soul,
It is well, with my soul,
It is well, it is well, with my soul.

Though Satan should buffet, though trials should come,
Let this blest assurance control,
That Christ has regarded my helpless estate,
And hath shed His own blood for my soul.

My sin, oh, the bliss of this glorious thought!
My sin, not in part but the whole,
Is nailed to the cross, and I bear it no more,
Praise the Lord, praise the Lord, O my soul!

For me, be it Christ, be it Christ hence to live:
If Jordan above me shall roll,
No pang shall be mine, for in death as in life
Thou wilt whisper Thy peace to my soul.

But, Lord, 'tis for Thee, for Thy coming we wait,
The sky, not the grave, is our goal;
Oh trump of the angel! Oh voice of the Lord!
Blessèd hope, blessèd rest of my soul!

And Lord, haste the day when my faith shall be sight,
The clouds be rolled back as a scroll;

The trump shall resound, and the Lord shall descend,
Even so, it is well with my soul.

It is well, with my soul,
It is well, with my soul,
It is well, it is well, with my soul.
(Horatio Gates Spafford, 1828-1888)

Letter 25

Behold the One Who Is Faithful to His Father

And a voice from heaven said, "This is my Son, whom I love; with him I am well pleased." Matthew 3:17

Dear Ones,

It is important to me that you understand *why* I know that I am absolutely secure in Christ, saved and safe for all eternity.

I understand that there are many warnings in the Bible, written to believers to keep us from taking grace for granted and making a mess of our lives. I need to heed these warnings, guarding my heart against secret sins, walking in wisdom, "proving" my salvation as I earnestly seek to live a Christ-honouring life. I know some people fear that believing in "eternal security" will make us lazy and soft on sin, but I think it can do the opposite. When we are safe and secure in Jesus, and know it, we can live valiantly for Jesus and wage war against sin and Satan with great courage and resolve.

Without question, the Bible teaches that a justified sinner is *kept* by the Lord, through thick and thin, good and bad, sunshine and rain, to be an exhibit of grace to the renown of the Lord.

> May God himself, the God of peace, sanctify you through and through. May your whole spirit, soul and body be kept blameless at the coming of our Lord Jesus Christ. The one who calls you is faithful, and he will do it. (1 Thessalonians 5:23, 24)

> In love he predestined us for adoption to sonship through Jesus Christ, in accordance with his pleasure and will—to the praise of his glorious grace, which he has freely given us in the One he loves. In

him we have redemption through his blood, the forgiveness of sins, in accordance with the riches of God's grace. (Ephesians 1:4-7)

While I could joyfully marshal countless Bible passages to encourage you to see and believe that if you truly cast yourself upon the Lord, you will be safe forever, what I want to do is take you right into the very secret counsels of God. I want us together to see that our security is fixed in the nature of God, rooted in the eternal community of joy we call the Trinity.

In John's Gospel, chapter six, Jesus takes us behind the scenes of salvation, into the precincts of the throne room. The following passage is one of the most precious in all the Bible, for therein Jesus tells us of a covenant between God the Father and God the Son. It is upon this covenant that our security rests.

> Then Jesus declared, "I am the bread of life. Whoever comes to me will never go hungry, and whoever believes in me will never be thirsty. But as I told you, you have seen me and still you do not believe. All those the Father gives me will come to me, and whoever comes to me I will never drive away. For I have come down from heaven not to do my will but to do the will of him who sent me. And this is the will of him who sent me, that I shall lose none of all those he has given me, but raise them up at the last day. For my Father's will is that everyone who looks to the Son and believes in him shall have eternal life, and I will raise them up at the last day." (John 6:35-40)

Do you see something wonderful happening between the Father and Son, something of which *you* are the beneficiary? Look with me:

* Jesus, the faithful Son, came to do His Father's will:
   For I have come down from heaven, not to do my
   will but to do the will of Him who sent Me.
* God the Father wants to see sinners saved:
   For my Father's will is that everyone who looks to
   the Son and believes in him shall have eternal life.

* God the Son also wants to see sinners saved:
     All those the Father gives me will come to me, and
     whoever comes to me I will never drive away.
* God the Father is "giving" sinners to Jesus, so that Jesus will
  save them:
     All those the Father gives me will come to me....
     that I shall lose none of all those he has given me.
* God the Son promises to save and keep each and every one that
  God the Father gives to Him:
     And this is the will of him who sent me, that I shall
     lose none of all those he has given me, but raise
     them up at the last day. For my Father's will is that
     everyone who looks to the Son and believes in him
     shall have eternal life, and I will raise them up at the
     last day.

Do you see the covenant here between the Father and the Son? It
is this covenant that secures the believer. Because Jesus is a faithful
Son, you and I are safe in our salvation. Hebrews tells us that:

> Christ is faithful as the Son over God's house (that's us!). And we are
> his house, if indeed we hold firmly to our confidence and the hope in
> which we glory. (Hebrews 3:6)

This covenant happens *outside* of you. It is not contingent upon
you. You did not initiate it. You could never have imagined it. You
cannot make it go away, nor can you enhance it. The Lord Jesus
knows full well the "project" the Father presented to Him when He
gave *you* to Him. Surely, the Father could have made it easier for
the Son by *not* doing so, but in order to display the incredible wonders of His grace, He freely, sovereignly chose to give *you* to Jesus,
and Jesus has welcomed you, and promises His Father to save and
keep you.

What a God! What a Gospel!

This grace-based, blood-secured covenant is the very centre of our salvation. From *our* standpoint, *we* "look to the Son," "come to the Son," "behold the Son." From God's standpoint, the Father gives us to the Son and the Son, being faithful to the Father, keeps us. We benefit from a promise made within the Trinity, sometime in eternity past:

> For he chose us in him before the creation of the world to be holy
> and blameless in his sight. In love he predestined us for adoption to
> sonship through Jesus Christ, in accordance with his pleasure and
> will—to the praise of his glorious grace, which he has freely given us
> in the One he loves. (Ephesians 1:4-6)

Jesus is the Good Shepherd (John 10:11) and the Captain of our Salvation (Hebrews 2:10, KJV). Focus your security outside of yourself, and upon the God—Father, Son, and Holy Spirit—who saves. Like me, you may be weak and failing, a faltering disciple on your best days, but Jesus is God's faithful Son. Behold Him and rest secure.

I offer you another hymn from the heart of William Cowper. This weak, frail Christian was and is proof positive that when Christ saves a sinner, He is faithful to keep him. Cowper struggled so deeply, yet Christ, the faithful Son, did not lose this one whom the Father had given for safekeeping:

****

There Is a Fountain

There is a fountain filled with blood drawn from Emmanuel's veins;
And sinners plunged beneath that flood lose all their guilty stains.
Lose all their guilty stains, lose all their guilty stains;
And sinners plunged beneath that flood lose all their guilty stains.

The dying thief rejoiced to see that fountain in his day;
And there have I, though vile as he, washed all my sins away.
Washed all my sins away, washed all my sins away;
And there have I, though vile as he, washed all my sins away.

Dear dying Lamb, Thy precious blood shall never lose its power
Till all the ransomed church of God be saved, to sin no more.
Be saved, to sin no more, be saved, to sin no more;
Till all the ransomed church of God be saved, to sin no more.

E'er since, by faith, I saw the stream Thy flowing wounds supply,
Redeeming love has been my theme, and shall be till I die.
And shall be till I die, and shall be till I die;
Redeeming love has been my theme, and shall be till I die.

Then in a nobler, sweeter song, I'll sing Thy power to save,
When this poor lisping, stammering tongue lies silent in the grave.
Lies silent in the grave, lies silent in the grave;
When this poor lisping, stammering tongue lies silent in the grave.

Lord, I believe Thou hast prepared, unworthy though I be,
For me a blood bought free reward, a golden harp for me!
'Tis strung and tuned for endless years, and formed by power divine,
To sound in God the Father's ears no other name but Thine.
(William Cowper, 1731-1800)

Letter 26

Behold the One Who Satisfies the Heart's Desire

I am the bread of life. John 6:35

Precious Family,

Augustine of Hippo (354-430), an early Church father in North Africa, is another one of my heroes. He was as wild and reprobate as ever a man was up until his thirtieth year, when he was gloriously converted. If it were possible to satisfy the human heart through sensuality, philosophy, and pleasure seeking, Augustine would have done so. But finding himself weary of godless living, Augustine was graciously saved by our Lord Jesus. Augustine later wrote these famous words:

> Thou hast made us for Thyself, o Lord, and our heart is restless until it finds its rest in Thee.

These days I am reading Eugene Peterson's, *A Long Obedience.* I find him to be a very helpful thinker and a stimulating writer. I think Augustine would say a hearty "amen" to Peterson's observation:

> A person has to be thoroughly disgusted with the way things are to find the motivation to set out on the Christian way. As long as we think the next election might eliminate crime and establish justice or another scientific breakthrough might save the environment or another pay raise might push us over the edge of anxiety into a life of tranquility, we are not likely to risk the arduous uncertainties of the life of faith. A person has to get fed up with the ways of the world before he, before she, acquires the appetite for the world of grace.[53]

I am discovering more of Jesus as I journey with Him. He is at the same time both the end of one journey and the beginning of another. He is the end of a journey in the sense that, when you have exhausted yourself on all the other options, and said a resolute "no" to the lie that is life without Christ, you find Christ. At that point, a new life journey begins, and Jesus is the end (in the sense of the goal) of this journey too. He is at the same time the divine satisfier, and the divine "*dis*-satisfier." Though my heart rests in Him, it is restless in Him. I have become at once at home and settled, and a stranger and pilgrim.

This is what Jesus does! The more complete I become in Him, the more I see the emptiness of "the world." I grow increasingly discontented with what I used to believe would satisfy.[54]

When Jesus tells us that He is the "Bread of Life," He is saying something about the deepest need of our hearts. He is speaking in a mini parable, for we all know what bread does. It *entices* (oh the smell of your mom's bread, hot out of the oven!) *nourishes,* and *satisfies.* But once you have had good bread, you have no use for bad bread. The point of the parable is not hard to see. Jesus entices, nourishes, satisfies, and dissatisfies at the critical basic "life" level, reachable only by Him.

I think I hear the challenge/invitation that Isaiah shouts to humanity everywhere and at all times:

> Come, all you who are thirsty, come to the waters; and you who have no money, come, buy and eat! Come, buy wine and milk without money and without cost. Why spend money on what is not bread, and your labor on what does not satisfy? Listen, listen to me, and eat what is good, and your soul will delight in the richest of fare. (Isaiah 55:1, 2)

Without question, my soul has found its home in Jesus. Yet my soul is homesick for Jesus. Children, I know that Jesus Christ is the answer to my deepest longings. I know that I was made for Him, and I will be dissatisfied and malnourished if I feed on anything or anyone else. I cannot expect *anything* or *anyone* to meet all my heart-needs. I have a God-shaped void within which only Christ can fill.[55] I now realize that my dreams demand eternity, for all of my "earthly" dreams have really been fulfilled, yet my heart still longs for...something. Christ, who has at the same time quieted me and stirred me to know His love, is the answer to the cries of my heart.

It is a huge relief to know that Jesus is the end of my old journey (call it my "journey of death"), and is the beginning of my new journey (call it my "journey of life"), and is the goal of my new journey (call it "life in fullness"). He feeds me the bread of life daily as I meet Him in His Word, and at the same time, He entices me with whiffs of something yet more wonderful that is being prepared for me. I sometimes can smell the bread of Heaven! I am now looking nowhere else but to Jesus for life. No other "gods"—earthly acclaim, status, creature comforts—can meet my heart-needs, for they are not so designed. I have tasted, even feasted at their tables and have always come away either hungry or sick to my stomach. Even human love (which I have experienced at its very best), as precious and right as it can be, if expected to feed the heart at the deepest level, fails and putrefies, for it is being asked to do what it is not designed to do.

When I was apprehended by Christ in 1975, I truly became enraptured by Him. Jesus became to me the Bread of Life and the Living Water. I became a Jesus-Follower and the Bible was the book that gave me Jesus. But! No sooner had I begun my journey than people began to lay all sorts of "Jesus *plus*" trips on me: "Jesus *plus* tongues," or "Jesus *plus* a certain version of the Bible," or "Jesus *plus* a certain view of the End Times," or "Jesus *plus* a 'blessing' from some 'anointed' person." But I must tell you, I never took the bait. I never ran after any of these enticements, because I had found the best in Jesus. I did not align myself with fads, movements, "blessings," or any other "thing," new or old, that people kept trying to heap upon me. Jesus has been the satisfaction and fascination of my mind, heart, and life since I met Him all those years ago. When you have met the Best, you simply do not want anything else. By God's grace I am, and shall always be, a Jesus person, plain and simple. Let others keep their "Jesus *plus*" trips to themselves!

Life begins when we say yes to Jesus and no to everything else. Strangely, in saying yes to Jesus, we are now at liberty to enjoy all in its proper, God-designed place. We do not become ascetics, but the freest, most satisfied people on earth. When we no longer expect anything this life has to offer to meet our deepest needs, this very life is transformed from black and white to full colour. It is in journeying with Jesus that the pilgrim-stranger learns to value and appreciate with total freedom the graces of everyday things, from the kiss of a spouse, to the smell of baked bread.

Walk with me as I follow Christ.

I'll leave you with a wondrous hymn. Even as I write, I can almost hear a great Welsh male voice choir singing:

****

Guide Me O Thou Great Jehovah

Guide me, O Thou great Jehovah,
Pilgrim through this barren land.
I am weak, but Thou art mighty;
Hold me with Thy powerful hand.
Bread of heaven, bread of heaven,
Feed me till I want no more;
Feed me till I want no more.

Open now the crystal fountain,
Where the living waters flow;
Let the river of salvation,
Follow all the desert through.

Strong Deliverer, strong Deliverer,
Be Thou still my Strength and Shield;
Be Thou still my Strength and Shield.

Lord, I trust Thy mighty power,
Wondrous are Thy works of old;
Thou deliver'st Thine from thraldom,
Who for nought themselves had sold:
Thou didst conquer, Thou didst conquer,
Sin, and Satan and the grave,
Sin, and Satan and the grave.

When I tread the verge of Jordan,
Bid my anxious fears subside;
Death of death and hell's destruction,
Land me safe on Canaan's side.
Songs of praises, songs of praises,
I will ever give to Thee;
I will ever give to Thee.

Musing on my habitation,
Musing on my heav'nly home,
Fills my soul with holy longings:
Come, my Jesus, quickly come;
Vanity is all I see;
Lord, I long to be with Thee!
Lord, I long to be with Thee!
(William Williams, 1717-1791)

Letter 27

Behold the One Who Baptizes You with His Holy Spirit

He will baptize you with the Holy Spirit and fire. Luke 3:16

Dear Children,

As I sit and write, the African rain is beating relentlessly upon the roof of my simple Rwandan shelter, somewhere in the mountains of this beautiful, Gospel-needy little land. In a few hours, I will be with a roomful of Rwandan pastors, hungry to learn. (I can hear them singing now from across the muddy yard, even over the sound of the pelting rain. What a heavenly sound they make! Heaven's choir will surely be African!) Soon I will traipse through the red mud to our classroom to be met by scores of bright eyes and dark faces, men and women ready to learn the things of God, and (of all things!) looking to *me* to teach them.

I need the Holy Spirit.

Now I know there are many views of how one is baptised in the Holy Spirit (or whatever you want to call it). I really do not have a view. Sorry. I never pitched up in any "Holy Spirit Camp." My theology in this regard is very simple. On this subject I have always been a bit of a "loner," never quite fitting in either with "charismatics" (who deemed me a Holy Spirit "quencher" because I did not exalt certain "gifts"), or "conservatives" (who deemed me to live on the charismatic edge of what is "safe," because I did not deny certain "gifts"). All I know is that I am nothing without divine empowerment, moment by moment. I cannot go before those African heroes and think clearly, be impassioned about truth, deal effectively with the Bible, or in any other way be useful to them, *unless the Holy Spirit empowers me.*

I have tended to look at it this way: I am nothing. I can accomplish nothing. But the Lord Jesus is wonderful, and desires to fill me with His own Spirit. If John 3:16 is God's promise to the *world*, then Luke 3:16 is God's promise to the *Church* (and Revelation 3:16 is God's warning to the Church if they ignore Luke 3:16...look it up...). I do not follow a stingy Jesus. He is abundant in grace for the needy. He is glad to give me His Holy Spirit generously:

> So I say to you: Ask and it will be given to you; seek and you will find; knock and the door will be opened to you. For everyone who asks receives; the one who seeks finds; and to the one who knocks, the door will be opened.
>
> Which of you fathers, if your son asks for a fish, will give him a snake instead? Or if he asks for an egg, will give him a scorpion? If you then, though you are evil, know how to give good gifts to your children, how much more will your Father in heaven give the Holy Spirit to those who ask him!" (Luke 11:9-13)

It is the heart of the Lord Jesus to give liberally of Himself to His people. Now, I understand that there are many who have a very tidy theology of just how the Lord works in terms of His Holy Spirit. Whole denominations have been founded upon particular views in regards to the Holy Spirit and His workings. Churches are established and then rent apart over disagreements concerning the precious Spirit of God!

I have always tried not to get involved in or sidetracked by such foolishness, but to remain focused on Christ and the Gospel, believing He is the whole point of the Holy Spirit's ministry in the first place. All I know is that I am nothing without everything God has for me. I want to live a life that brings glory to the Lord Jesus, and I cannot do this without the ongoing help of the Holy Spirit. I pray constantly for a filling, a baptism of the Holy Spirit. I go forth in trembling weakness, looking to Him to enable me. Time and time again, the Lord Jesus fills me with His Holy Spirit and empowers me, little old *me,* to minister the wonders of Him.

I would advise you to look beyond superficial "signs" for the "fullness of the Spirit" (i.e. tongues). The best teachings on sure signs of the presence and ministry of the Holy Spirit I ever read are in two essays, one by A.W. Tozer called, "How to Try a Spirit," and the other by Jonathan Edwards called, "The Distinguishing Marks of a Work of the Spirit." Both of these spiritual giants basically say the same thing, and I have blended the two together as follows:

The sure signs that God's Holy Spirit is at work are:

*An increased love for Jesus Christ among God's People

*An increased love for truth—the Bible—among God's People

*An increased hatred for sin in all forms among God's People

*An increased love for the Church among God's People

*An increased love for the lost and for mission among God's People

I don't think you can do better than to beseech God to pour out His Holy Spirit upon you and your work, to the end that the five trademarks above are evident in all your endeavours.

My advice to you is that you do not allow yourself to get embroiled in silly debates over how the Holy Spirit works. Rather, spend that time otherwise wasted, on your knees asking God to empower you so that you can go forth and glorify His Son. Pound on Heaven's gates and seek power from on high, and you shall not be denied. The key to fullness is to recognize emptiness. It matters not a whiff if you were "baptized in the Holy Spirit" five years ago. What matters is, are you filled *today*?

Well, I am off to trudge through the mud to teach a roomful of hungry pastors. Jesus will not let me down. He promises power to this weak man, that He may be glorified in these days.

Edwin Hatch was a good and godly minister, but he became aware of a lack in his ministry and meetings. He sought the Lord for new fullness and found it. In the old days, we used to sing this great hymn...maybe one day we will be humble enough to sing it again:

****

Breathe on Me Breath of God

Breathe on me, breath of God,
Fill me with life anew,
That I may love what Thou dost love,
And do what Thou wouldst do.

Breathe on me, breath of God,
Until my heart is pure,
Until with Thee I will one will,
To do and to endure.

Breathe on me, breath of God,
Blend all my soul with Thine,
Until this earthly part of me
Glows with Thy fire divine.

Breathe on me, breath of God,
So shall I never die,
But live with Thee the perfect life
Of Thine eternity.
(Edwin Hatch, 1835-1889)

Letter 28

Behold Him Who Delights in Doing You Good

And we know that in all things God works for the good of those who love him, who have been called according to his purpose.
Romans 8:28

Dearest Ones,

One of the most precious times I had as a father was a night I spent in a hospital a few years ago with our dear Katherine. Having just returned from Africa, she was in the tortures of an inflamed pancreas. How she was suffering! Together, we alighted upon Song of Songs 7:10:

> I belong to my beloved, and his desire is for me.

I remember so fondly and well how Katherine held fast to that great truth as pain gripped her. The wonder of the passionate love of Jesus was a source of strength and joy in the midst of pain and concern. God was actually *doing good* to us in the midst of a real trial. He was manifesting His impassioned heart to us on a hospital ward.

Christian history is bristling with the biographies of men and women who have discovered the joys of a God who delights to do them good, even in the midst of the most severe trials. Next to the Bible, I have enjoyed and benefited from reading biographies of ordinary folks who have followed Jesus, discovering His constant goodness towards them amidst the tribulations of life. I could tell you stories all night. (I often have!) It is good to recount the tales of real people who have discovered the truth that God is doing good to them through *all* the seasons of their lives. Go and read the lives of

Adoniram Judson, Amy Carmichael, Benjamin and Annie Warfield, Hudson Taylor, C.T. Studd, Madame Guyon, Mary Slessor, John Calvin—the list goes on and on.

I have time and desire now only to recount the story of one to whom God did good through the severest of trials. I speak of my dear friend, Nathan Fisher. You all know him, but I know him so well. He was my theological sparring partner, my brother, my confidant, and my dear friend. I was thirty, he seventeen when we first crossed paths. I was a pastor, he was a dope-smoking tearaway. Jesus apprehended him (this is called *irresistible grace*!). He and his young wife, Sonja, came through thoroughly for Jesus. I am not sure I ever saw such a complete conversion. He was a builder—tough as nails. He started taking his Bible to the worksite, and as the others were reading porn at lunch, Nathan was immersed in the Word. (You can imagine the scene...)

As he began to discern a call to the ministry, he and his wife discussed and prayed through the meaning and cost of such a call upon a young family. Nathan took the plunge and immersed himself in study. He developed the finest theological mind with which I personally ever engaged. I mean this. We met often to discuss the things of God. He could outdo me at almost every turn, this weight-lifting man's man of a theologian. I always knew before any meeting with him (usually at McDonald's) that he was going ask me: "What are you reading?" I also knew I had better have a good answer. Pastors who did not read pained him!

I remember so clearly the day we met for lunch for the last time. He told me of an abscess in his mouth: "But I know it is more than that," he said. "I know it is cancer." A fourteen-hour operation soon followed, and then a year of unbearable physical pain for him and emotional pain for his dear family. I was privileged to coach Nathan around the last lap of his life. We had so many precious times together, I sitting on his hospital bed, he with what remained of his head bandaged, instructing me in the things of God. We would weep and laugh. More than once, he told me that he was "in green pastures."

The last week of his young life, I asked him a straightforward question:

"Nathan, if you could turn the clock back a year, and again be your strident, muscular, able self, or be here now, the man that you are...which would you choose?"

Without hesitation, my brother said, "I would never want to go back. I know God, the things of God, as I never have before." He then took me to 1 Peter 4:1..."he who has suffered in his body is done with sin."

"Brother," he said, "there were sins in my life that I always struggled with. Not anymore. I would not go back to those struggles. God has been good to me. The only sin I struggle with now is impatience. I want to go on and be with Jesus."

Nathan died in triumph, a man done with sin, chastened and loved by Jesus, ready to go home. It is hard not to cry as I write these words. I can tell you that for all the pain Nathan and his family endured, God was good to him, and I am confident that in time, his family will be able to testify (if not already) of His goodness to them all.

Children, God delights in doing good to those who love Him. This is not expressed so much on the sunny days as on the cloudy days. In 1758, Jonathan Edwards died unexpectedly of a smallpox vaccine gone wrong, leaving his wife and eleven children behind. His wife, Sarah, received the news by mail. Hear the words of Sarah, written in a letter to her daughter:

> What shall I say: A holy and good God has covered us with a dark cloud. O that we may kiss the rod, and lay our hands on our mouths! The Lord has done it. He has made me adore his goodness that we had him so long. But my God lives; and he has my heart. O what a legacy my husband, and your father, has left to us! We are all given to God: and there I am and love to be. Your ever affectionate mother, Sarah Edwards.[56]

It is my prayer for you that you will know and experience the God who delights to do good to you. Yes, I pray that you will have many sunny days. I have had so many! I pray that you will be spared the many evils and trials familiar to the fallen sons of Adam. But I also pray that you, my dear, dear children, will know the character of God in such a way that, when dark clouds pass overhead, you will realize that He, in His loving providence, is doing good to you, producing some choice fruit in you that can only grow in a valley.

Joseph Scriven gave us one of the most famous and precious hymns of all time. What few of us know is that this great hymn of comfort was birthed in a life of almost unimaginable trial:[57]

****

What a Friend We Have in Jesus

What a friend we have in Jesus,
all our sins and griefs to bear!
What a privilege to carry
everything to God in prayer!
O what peace we often forfeit,
O what needless pain we bear,
all because we do not carry
everything to God in prayer.

Have we trials and temptations?
Is there trouble anywhere?
We should never be discouraged;
take it to the Lord in prayer.
Can we find a friend so faithful
who will all our sorrows share?
Jesus knows our every weakness;
take it to the Lord in prayer.

Are we weak and heavy laden,
cumbered with a load of care?
Precious Savior, still our refuge;
take it to the Lord in prayer.
Do thy friends despise, forsake thee?
Take it to the Lord in prayer!
In his arms he'll take and shield thee;
thou wilt find a solace there.
(Joseph Scriven, 1819-1886)

Letter 29

Behold Him Who Is Your Rest

There remains, then, a Sabbath-rest for the people of God.
Hebrews 4:9

Dear Ones,

Your dad was a striver. For numerous reasons, I have spent much of my life striving to prove myself, accomplish the extraordinary, be seen to be somebody. What an intolerable burden! Idols are very hard taskmasters, and the idol of self-accomplishment is perhaps the cruelest of all. I served him for years.

Your dear mother saw this in me long before I did (she has always been able to see right through me). Many, many times this godly woman waited in silence, pouring out her heart to God, that He would bring me to a place of rest in Him. She never rebuked me for my self-absorption (though she could have!), but just loved me, saw the good (however buried beneath layers of self), and trusted the Lord to do His work. She is without a doubt, the true hero of this family, and without question the godliest person I have ever known. If any of you have not come to see this by now, you are sure to one day.

Just because someone is a follower of Jesus, does not mean he immediately ceases his striving! He may very well simply channel his striving into ministry. Many do. I have. Perhaps those of us in ministry of one form or another are vexed more than most by the idol of self-accomplishment. To be seen as the one who prays the most, gets up the earliest, reads the most, preaches the most anointed sermons (I almost wrote "annoying" sermons), walks in the greatest humility (talk about twisted!)—such are the hellish pitfalls of the earnest.

I have had to ask the Lord Jesus to forgive me of bad motives, much self, so much striving...all ostensibly in His service. He has allowed me to crash and burn on the rocks of my own accomplishments, only to bring me to a place of rest in Him. What a gracious and wonderful God we have!

I am coming to learn late what I want you to learn early: That we are to rest our souls in Jesus. He is not impressed by us. He has seen and heard all the great preachers, pray-ers, and missionaries. Although impossible to impress, He is easy to please. He is overjoyed by us when we simply bow and exalt Him. Be careful of your flight status, your upgrades, your full calendars, your being in demand, your amazing kids. "But God forbid that I should glory, save in the cross of our Lord Jesus Christ, by whom the world has been crucified unto me, and I unto the world" (Galatians 6:14, KJV). Very quickly, you can get a sort of spiritual vertigo, and down you will go! "Woe be unto you when all men speak well of you." For the servant of Jesus, success is much harder on the soul than opposition. The fat times are a far greater danger than the lean.

The letter to the Hebrews tells us that our Sabbath is no longer really a *day,* but a *person.* Our rest is Jesus Himself, and His Gospel. The *day* is a shadow, the *person* the reality. (I believe we should keep the shadow/day as a statement that we have found the reality/person. You will do well to heed my advice.) In the Gospel, we *cease striving.* We rest in the truth that we are justified by grace through faith alone and not by ministry, perceived spirituality, reputation, weariness, influence, or anything else. It is amazing just how strongly we are hardwired by sin to try to justify ourselves, to prove our worth. I sometimes think the Lord looks at us and with a compassionate shake of His head says, "My poor, exhausted, striving child, I am not asking you to kill yourself trying to prove yourself. You really are getting in my way, for I would like to use you for my glory, and if you do not heed the gentle promptings of my Spirit to rest in the Gospel, I am going to have to reduce you. I am seeing too much of the *young* man, too much of the *old* man, but not enough of the *new* man when I look at you!"

The wisdom of John the Baptiser has really spoken to me since my nervous breakthrough a few years ago. (Jake was there, holding me when the dam burst. Then followed a month or two in my pajamas…It is amazing what that can do for your soul.) In John 3, JB's church is shrinking and JC's is growing. This would be bad news for a striver, but great news for a true servant of the Lord:

> To this John replied: "A person can receive only what is given them from heaven (John, in context, is talking specifically about size and prestige of ministry)….The friend who attends the bridegroom waits and listens for him, and is full of joy when he hears the bridegroom's voice. That joy is mine, and it is now complete. He must become greater; I must become less." (John 3:27-30)

Dear child, learn of Jesus, for His yoke is easy and His burden is light. It is in Him that you will find rest for your souls. Learn to submit to His Lordship, to harbour your spirit in His Gospel. Receive the ministry and life He gives you as "from above" and run with it, but do not strive for what is not ordained to be yours.

> My heart is not proud, Lord, my eyes are not haughty; I do not concern myself with great matters or things too wonderful for me.
> But I have calmed and quieted myself, I am like a weaned child with its mother; like a weaned child I am content.
> Israel, put your hope in the Lord both now and forevermore.
> (Psalm 131)

I want to leave you with the great words of a long forgotten hymn. Humble Christians used to sing these words. Maybe one day we will again (Oh, the soul poverty born of our pride!):

****

Dear Lord and Father of Mankind [58]

Dear Lord and Father of mankind,
forgive our foolish ways;
reclothe us in our rightful mind,
in purer lives thy service find,
in deeper reverence, praise.

In simple trust like theirs who heard,
beside the Syrian sea,
the gracious calling of the Lord,
let us, like them, without a word,
rise up and follow thee.

O sabbath rest by Galilee,
O calm of hills above,
where Jesus knelt to share with thee
the silence of eternity,
interpreted by love!

Drop thy still dews of quietness,
till all our strivings cease;
take from our souls the strain and stress,
and let our ordered lives confess
the beauty of thy peace.

Breathe through the heats of our desire
thy coolness and thy balm;
let sense be dumb, let flesh retire;
speak through the earthquake, wind, and fire,
O still, small voice of calm.
(John Greenleaf Whittier, 1807-1892)

Letter 30

Behold Him Who Summons Your Highest Praise

Then I heard every creature in heaven and on earth and under
the earth and on the sea, and all that is in them, saying:
"To him who sits on the throne and to the Lamb be praise and
honor and glory and power, for ever and ever!"
The four living creatures said, "Amen," and the elders fell down
and worshiped. Revelation 5:13, 14

Dearest Children,

C.S Lewis observed that *praise* is the consummation of *joy.* He was
right (as usual).

What he meant was this: The experience of joy, as wonderful as it
is, is not fulfilled until the source of it is praised. For instance, when
mom produces one of her amazing pizzas, we all experience the joy
of sitting together and devouring it. But it is when we praise her for
her skill, love, and efforts that the circle is complete and the joy is
consummated. Likewise, think of the last time you were overjoyed
at a sporting event or a concert. The action on the field or the music
on the stage brought such joy to your heart that it would have been
impossible not to erupt in praise. Imagine the ridiculous scene of a
stadium full of fans, expressing their joy...by sitting still and silent!

I remember seeing Paul McCartney and Wings in 1976 in
Cleveland. I managed fifth row seats at the Cleveland Coliseum. The
atmosphere was electric with anticipation. I can distinctly remember
deciding that because I was so cool, *I* would not get caught up in
the event, and no one was going to catch me in any expression of
"Beatlemania." Well, no sooner had Paul and company walked on
stage then my concern for image was suddenly gone, and the joy of

my heart was being duly consummated with very uncool jumping up
and down, and screaming. I think I did the same at a Doobie Brothers
concert in 1977. Those were the days!

Here is my point: We were meant to be creatures of praise. We were
made to love beauty and express our joyful admiration with all of our
being. Remember Henry Scougal's observation that the health of a soul
is determined by the value of what it loves. The more excellent the object
of our praise, the better off our souls will be. (I am not sure what this says
about me in relation to the Doobie Brothers.) Finally, we were created
to praise the most beautiful "thing" of all...the Lord Himself. The theme
of Heaven will be the eternal praise of the Triune God. The immensity
of our salvation (currently being appreciated only in part), and the joy
which it produces will be expressed in the only way appropriate: The
pure praise of God—the Father, the Son, and the Holy Spirit.

We must not—we dare not—wait for Heaven to begin a life of
praise to the Lord Jesus. As dim as our understanding may be this
side of eternity, we must stir up our spirits to consider the wonders
of our salvation and *begin* to offer the praise due to Jesus Christ *now*.
If there is any experience of Gospel joy within, there must be an
expression of praise without.

> Praise the Lord!
> For it is good to sing praises to our God;
> For it is pleasant *and* praise is becoming. (Psalm 147:1, NASB)

> I will give thanks to you, Lord, with all my heart;
> I will tell of all your wonderful deeds.
> I will be glad and rejoice in you;
> I will sing the praises of your name, O Most High. (Psalm 9:1)

> Deliver me from the guilt of bloodshed, O God,
> you who are God my Savior,
> and my tongue will sing of your righteousness.
> Open my lips, Lord,
> and my mouth will declare your praise. (Psalm 51:14, 15)

I think praise is not only the Christian's duty and proper response to the grace of God, I think it is his secret weapon. I just do not think Satan can abide it. When a dear saint, be him or her ever so battered by the evil one, recalls the saving grace of God upon his soul and offers up a sacrifice of praise, the enemy seems to have no staying power. This is spiritual warfare at the elite troop level. This honours God and the Gospel and displays a true sense of spiritual maturity and discipline.

In 2 Chronicles 20, Jehoshaphat and the people of God were up against it with the Moabites. God gave the king grace to lead His people well, and the key to their victory was spiritual and rooted in their praise of God:

> Early in the morning they left for the Desert of Tekoa. As they set out, Jehoshaphat stood and said, "Listen to me, Judah and people of Jerusalem! Have faith in the Lord your God and you will be upheld; have faith in his prophets and you will be successful." After consulting the people, Jehoshaphat appointed men to sing to the Lord and to praise him for the splendor of his holiness as they went out at the head of the army, saying:
>
> "Give thanks to the Lord,
>
> for his love endures forever."
>
> As they began to sing and praise, the Lord set ambushes against the men of Ammon and Moab and Mount Seir who were invading Judah, and they were defeated.
> (2 Chronicles 20:20-22)

Learn sooner than I did to live a *life* of praise to Jesus for who He is, what He has done, what He is sure to do, and you will honour God, defeat your adversary, and bless those around you.

Well, neither the Doobies nor the Beatles could ever write a song with eight verses. It takes a nobler theme to produce nobler praise! Don't rush over these words, but let them be a help to you in your worship of Him who alone is worthy of our highest praise:

****

When Morning Gilds the Skies

When morning gilds the skies,
My heart awaking cries,
May Jesus Christ be praised!
Alike at work and prayer
To Jesus I repair;
May Jesus Christ be praised!

Whene'er the sweet church bell
Peals over hill and dell,
May Jesus Christ be praised!
Oh,hark to what it sings,
As joyously it rings,
May Jesus Christ be praised!

My tongue shall never tire
Of chanting with the choir,
May Jesus Christ be praised!
This song of sacred joy,
It never seems to cloy,
May Jesus Christ be praised!

When sleep her balm denies,
My silent spirit sighs,
May Jesus Christ be praised!
When evil thoughts molest,
With this I shield my breast,
May Jesus Christ be praised!

Does sadness fill my mind?
A solace here I find,
May Jesus Christ be praised!
Or fades my earthly bliss?
My comfort still is this,
May Jesus Christ be praised!

The night becomes as day,
When from the heart we say,
May Jesus Christ be praised!
The powers of darkness fear,
When this sweet chant they hear,
May Jesus Christ be praised!

In heaven's eternal bliss
The loveliest strain is this,
May Jesus Christ be praised!
Let earth, and sea, and sky,
From depth to height, reply,
May Jesus Christ be praised!

Be this, while life is mine,
My canticle divine,
May Jesus Christ be praised!
Be this the eternal song
Through ages all along,
May Jesus Christ be praised!
(Ancient German hymn, translated to
English in 1854 by Edward Caswall)

A Good-Night Song

Dearest Children,

It has been a joy to write these simple letters to you, and it is my prayer that Jesus Christ will be the treasure and joy of your lives until we are all joined together before Him in Heaven.

How quickly these years have flown by! How fondly your mother and I remember those wondrous nights when you were all tucked-up in your beds, safe in our home, while I sat in the hallway playing my guitar to you, singing simple songs of faith as you drifted off to sleep. Now, as then, I offer these words to you, sung first by your mother when you were infants in her arms, praying them over your lives, the lives of your children, and the lives of generations yet to come, until Jesus returns:

> The steadfast love of the Lord never ceases;—
>> his mercies never come to an end;
> they are new every morning;
>> great is your faithfulness.
>> (Lamentations 3:22-23) (ESV)

Sweet Dreams,

Your Father
Overland Park, Kansas
May 2013

Postscript

Twenty-Five Books That Have Shaped My Life

These come in no particular order!

George Whitefield: The Life and Times of the Great Evangelist of the 18th Century by Arnold Dallimore.

Through Gates of Splendor by Elizabeth Elliot

Hudson Taylor's Spiritual Secret by Howard Taylor *

The Complete Works of Francis Schaeffer, Volumes 1-5 by Francis Schaeffer

The Knowledge of the Holy by A.W. Tozer *

Knowing God by J.I. Packer

The Cross of Christ by John Stott

Evidence That Demands a Verdict by Josh McDowell

Mere Christianity by C.S. Lewis

The Cost of Discipleship by Dietrich Bonhoeffer

True Discipleship by William McDonald

Why Revival Tarries by Leonard Ravenhill

The Forgotten Spurgeon by Iain Murray

The Life of God in the Soul of Man by Henry Scougal

Matthew Henry's Commentary on the Whole Bible by Matthew Henry *

The Works of Jonathan Edwards by Jonathan Edwards

Future Grace by John Piper

C.T. *Studd* by Norman Grubb

On Giants' Shoulders by J. I. Packer

Jonathan Edwards by Iain Murray

Grudem's Systematic Theology by Wayne Grudem

The Pursuit of God by A.W. Tozer

The Saint's Everlasting Rest by Richard Baxter

Heaven by Randy Alcorn

Preaching and Preachers by Martyn Lloyd-Jones

Kids, you can see by this list that I am not a front row scholar by any means. I love to read books written by men and women whose hearts burn for Jesus. While I could fill pages with book titles, if one set out to work through this list, in the end they would have a solid theological base, and I predict, a burning heart. I have also always tried to read histories, novels, sciences—anything to help my brain work—always asking Jesus to help me remember what I have read.

Mom also has always had her nose in a book. Alas, if we weren't such readers, we probably would have had ten kids instead of just you seven!

From Mom: Most of my reading has been either to help my personal walk with the Lord, or my everyday life in the family. These are some that have had a powerful and lasting effect on my inner motivations and Christian philosophy of living. There are probably other key ones, but my memory is not like Dad's! Mostly, I have tried to read God's Word as a priority—READ it over and over—thoroughly and devotionally; meditate on it and pray to live it (Psalm 119)!

Below are **Books That Have Shaped My Life**: (* above as well)

The Cross and the Switchblade by David Wilkerson

Ministering to the Lord by Roxanne Brant

The Disciplined Life by Richard Shelley Taylor

Freedom of Simplicity; Celebration of Discipline by Richard Foster

Abide in Me; Absolute Surrender; Like Christ; Divine Healing
How to Raise your Children for Christ (and others) by Andrew Murray

The Normal Christian Life by Watchman Nee

The Practice of the Presence of God by Brother Lawrence

The Art of Homemaking by Edith Schaeffer

A Mother's Time by Elise Arndt

Biographies of Susanna Wesley and Abraham Lincoln (my hero as a child)

Notes

[1] Mom still loves to throw me over her shoulder and carry me off upstairs...

[2] Your grandfather Gillespie, my father, was at Buchenwald on April 11, the day it was liberated. Had the Allies been just a little sooner, Bonhoeffer would have survived.

[3] Christopher Lydon, http://www.radioopensource.org/martin-martys-saint- for-moderns-dietrich-bonhoeffer/

[4] Thankfully it has been reduced to a readable 80,000!

[5] I have been told that John Newton was still a slave trader when he wrote these words. What a gracious, patient Saviour we have! He begins a work of grace in us when we are such miserable sinners!

[6] How I love that quote from Erasmus, that the Bible "will give Christ to you in an intimacy so close that he would be less visible to you if he stood before your eyes" (From John Stott *The Incomparable Christ* (Nottingham: IVP,2001), 15.

[7] I have listed twenty-five books which have had an impact on my life as a *postscript* to these letters.

[8] So when the devil throws your sins in your face and declares that you deserve death and hell, tell him this: 'I admit that I deserve death and hell, what of it? For I know One who suffered and made satisfaction on my behalf. His name is Jesus Christ, Son of God, and where He is there I shall be also!'" Martin Luther http://www.goodreads.com/author/quotes/29874.Martin_Luther

"Learn to know Christ and him crucified. Learn to sing to him, and say, 'Lord Jesus, you are my righteousness, I am your sin. You have taken upon yourself what is mine and given me what is yours. You have become what you were not so that I might become what I was not.'" Martin Luther http://dailychristianquote.com/dcqluther.html

[9] Charlotte Elliott was a pain-racked invalid for most of her life. When asked by a godly houseguest if she was truly a Christian, she curtly replied that she did not want to talk about it. Upon reflection, she later enquired how she, a fearful, weak, doubting sinner could ever come to Christ, to which the wise guest replied "Why not come just as you are?" Those words of grace opened the way to Heaven for her, and, in coming to Christ, this trembling believer wrote the hymn that has helped untold thousands come to Jesus "just as they are." See http://www.stempublishing.com/hymns/biographies/elliott.html.

[10] Cited in Kevin Belmonte, *Miraculous* (Nashville: Thomas Nelson,2012), 65.

[11] Wayne Grudem, *Systematic Theology*, (Nottingham: IVP, 1994), 226.

[12] It was GK Chesterton who observed that we have misplaced our humility. It belongs on us, but we have put it on our beliefs. We should be humble (unsure) in regard to ourselves, but confident in regard to what we believe. Instead, we are confident in ourselves and unsure about what we believe. BACKWARDS!

[13] Cited in Eugene Peterson *A Long Obedience in the Same Direction* (Downers Grove: IVP,2000), 36.

[14] "O For a Thousand Tongues to Sing." The original hymn had eighteen verses. Go to http://en.wikipedia.org/wiki/O_for_a_Thousand_Tongues_to_Sing to feast on all of them!

[15] "I am more afraid of my own heart than of the pope and all his cardinals. I have within me the great pope, Self." Martin Luther http://www.brainyquote.com/quotes/authors/m/martin_luther.html#i8Yjumvq7Lv0kcrF.99

[16] http://www.orlutheran.com/html/luthbibl.html

[17] This is the first known use of "torbid" in the English language. I know because I just made it up. It means "necrotic to the point of putrescence."

[18] I am quoting this from memory, and cannot find the source reference. It is well-known that the remorseful Wilde called for a priest at the close of his life, and was given a Catholic burial.

[19] Although not perhaps as famous as his brother, John, being filled to overflowing with the wonders of God's love, he penned between six and seven *thousand* hymns. What a heart filled with grace from Him who is "full of grace and truth"!

[20] C.S. Lewis, Prince Caspian: The Return to Narnia *The Chronicles of Narnia* (Hew York: Harper Collins, 1994), p.141.

[21] John Stott rightly describes God's wrath: "It is never unpredictable, but always predictable, because it is provoked by evil and evil alone. The wrath of God...is his steady, unrelenting, unremitting, uncompromising antagonism to evil in all its forms and manifestations." John Stott, *The Cross of Christ* (Leicester: IVP, 1986), 173.

[22] See for example: Matthew 5:12; 16:27; 1 Corinthians 3:14; Colossians 3:24, and; Hebrews 11:26.

[23] Jonathan Edwards spoke of eternity as an ocean of joy into which each child of grace is cast, each one being like a vessel, filled to capacity with joy, although vessels were not all the same size. What we did with grace in this life determines our capacity for joy in Jesus in the next life. How "large" will you be in Eternity?

[24] Henry Scougal, *The life of God in the Soul of Man* (Geanies House: Christian Focus Publications , 1996), 73,74.

[25] I first heard this poem as a very young Christian in 1976, on Phil Keaggy's album, *Love Broke Through*. His rendition is masterful. For the complete text, see C.S.Lewis *Poems, Harvest Books, 1992*.

[26] It was the godly and manly Rev. Jeff Sharp, of Plymouth Methodist Central Hall who told me this quote while we were on our way to a prayer meeting in 1988. I went straight home and wrote it in my journal. I have no other source for it.

[27] Elizabeth Elliot, *Amy Carmichael, Her Life and Legacy* (Eastbourne: Kingsway Publications, 1987), 221. Poem is in public domain.

[28] C.S. Lewis *God In The Dock, Christian Apologetics* (Grand Rapids: Wm. B. Eerdmans, 1970), 100.

[29] My credo, when boiled down, is really very simple: 1) Truth *exists* (though it is fashionable these days to say that there is no such a thing); 2) Truth is *knowable* (though it is fashionable today to exalt ignorance as a virtue); 3) Jesus Christ *is* truth (an absolutely radical assertion in today's culture), and; 4) The Bible is a *faithful witness* to Jesus Christ, the truth (a necessary conclusion if the first three are true). These four convictions are enough to get you martyred in the East or marginalized in the West. Marginalized is worse...

[30] Eric Metaxas, *Bonhoeffer: Pastor, Martyr, Prophet Spy.* (Nashville: Thomas Nelson Publishers), 2010.

[31] Eugene Peterson, *The Message* (Colorado Springs: NavPress, 2002), 1481.

[32] Have you seen those "cute" little t-shirts that sentimental parents adorn their infants in: "God's little angel," and such? How about a *biblical* t-shirt for the little rebels: "By nature an object of wrath" or "conceived in iniquity"!

[33] For the amazing story of how this hymn came to be, go to http://www.tanbible.com/tol_sng/sng_theloveofgod.htm

[34] http://www.johnowen.org/quotes/

[35] Corrie Ten Boom, quoted in Peter J. Kreeft, *The Philosophy of Tolkien* (San Francisco: Ignatius Press, 2005), 186.

[36] I met a new hero today while reading Metaxas' *Bonhoeffer*. Henning von Tresckow was arrested for his part in the 1944 plot to kill Hitler. A Christian, he bravely took his own life rather than be tortured and forced to reveal the names of other conspirators. Just before he died he said: "A human being's moral integrity begins when he is prepared to sacrifice his life for his convictions." Metaxas *op.cit.* p. 482.

[37] "John Owen, probably the most prominent and respected academic leader of Bunyan's own era, once went to hear Bunyan preach. Charles II, hearing of it, asked the learned doctor of divinity why someone as thoroughly educated as he would want to hear a mere tinker preach. Owen replied, "May it please your Majesty, if I could possess the tinker's abilities to grip men's hearts, I would gladly give in exchange all my learning." http://www.patheos.com/blogs/adrianwarnock/2007/10/john-owen-and-charles-spurgeon-on-john/

[38] http://www.desiringgod.org/resource-library/biographies/to-live-upon-god-that-is-invisible

[39] cited in http://www.oocities.org/weprotest.geo/luther.html

[40] Many times in the New Testament, the Greek word *skandalon* (scandal) is used to describe the Gospel, i.e.Galatians 5:11, which the NIV translates as *offence.*

[41] Arnold Dallimore, *George Whitefield* (Westchester: Cornerstone Books, 1979, Vol 1), 60. Leonard Ravenhill recommended this great biography to me. I read it in 1982-83, and it proved to be vital in my deliverance from Charles Finney and my subsequent spiritual formation.

[42] Cited in http://enrichmentjournal.ag.org/199704/078_whitefield.cfm

[43] *ibid.*

[44] "The devil sought to discourage (Luther), by making him feel guilty, through rehearsing a list of his sins. When the devil had finished, Luther purportedly said, 'Think harder: you must have forgotten some.' And the devil did think, and he listed more sins. When he was done enumerating the sins, Luther said, 'Now, with a red pen write over that list, 'The blood of Jesus Christ, God's Son, cleanses us from all sin.' The devil had nothing to say...Luther writes:

'Christ, when tempted by the Devil, responded by throwing the words of sacred Scripture at him. His defense was an offensive proclamation of truth. The best response of any disciple of Jesus is to take the offensive and speak the words of eternal life into the darkness.'" cited in http://www.redeemer-lutheran.net/Articles/1000039345/Redeemer_Lutheran_Church/Media_Center/Pastors_Articles/Throwing_Ink_at.aspx

[45] http://en.wikipedia.org/wiki/Anthony_Ashley-Cooper,_7th_Earl_of_Shaftesbury

[46] http://www.cmalliance.org/about/beliefs/coming-king

[47] Harry Young, the late father of Dee Molton. Harry, a stout Irish boxer turned missionary, died from a heart attack while teaching a Bible study to a gathering of Muslims. It just does not get better than that!

[48] Have a look at these powerful passages: Mark 13:32-37; 1 Thessalonians 4:13-18; 2 Corinthians 5:6-8, and; Philippians 1:20.

[49] This is what offends me the most regarding the "prosperity 'gospel.'" Jesus is not the *end* but the *means* to the end, which is personal wealth. How offensive!

[50] John Piper, *The Pleasures of God* (Geanies House: Christian Focus, 1998), 269. Piper tells that just before her death, Mary "spoke these incredible words: 'I do not regret leaving home and friends. If I had it to do over, I would do it with more pleasure, yes, with all my heart.'" *Ibid.* p.270.

[51] http://en.wikipedia.org/wiki/John_Gibson_Paton

[52] http://en.wikipedia.org/wiki/Europe

[53] Peterson, *A Long Obedience,* 25.

[54] C.S Lewis wrote: "If we find ourselves with a desire that nothing in this world can satisfy, the most probable explanation is that we were made for another world."

[55] Blaise Paschal (1623-1662)

[56] http://www.enjoyinggodministries.com/article/33-cheerful-resignation-to-the-divine-will-learning-from-the-death-of-jonathan-edwards/ Sarah herself would die just a few months later of dysentery at the age of 48.

[57] "Joseph Scriven was born in 1819 of prosperous parents in Dublin, Ireland. He was a graduate of Trinity College. At the age of 25, he decided to leave his native country and migrate to Canada. His reasons for leaving his country seem to be two-fold: the religious influence of the Plymouth Brethren upon his life estranging him from his family. His fiancée accidentally drowned in 1845, the night before they were to be married.The grief-stricken young man moved to Canada. There he again fell in love, was due to be married and the young woman suddenly fell ill of pneumonia and died. He then devoted the rest of his life to helping others.

In 1855, while staying with companion Mr. James Sackville, he received news from Ireland of his mother being terribly ill. He wrote a poem to comfort his mother called "Pray Without Ceasing." It was later set to music and renamed... becoming the hymn "What a Friend we Have in Jesus" Joseph did not have any intentions nor dream that his poem would be for publication in the newspaper and later becoming a favorite hymn among the millions of Christians around the world." http://en.wikipedia.org/wiki/Joseph_M._Scriven

[58] This amazing hymn is just a portion of a much longer poem "The Brewing of Soma," an exposure of religious fanaticism. The poem resolves itself in the stanzas that have become this precious hymn.